HERO IN THE WORKPLACE

JONATHAN FISH

Copyright © 2017 Jonathan Fish.

All rights reserved. No part of this book may be used or reproduced by any means, graphic, electronic, or mechanical, including photocopying, recording, taping or by any information storage retrieval system without the written permission of the author except in the case of brief quotations embodied in critical articles and reviews.

Published by The Ghost Publishing

Dedication

To my parents for their love and guidance and for instilling in me the confidence it takes to tackle extremely complex situations.

To my wife and children who allow me go out in the middle of the night on emergencies, thanks for your understanding that it's a 24-hour job.

Also to my employees and co-workers who have worked extremely hard to make National Water Restoration a success. I certainly could not have done this without every one of you.

CONTENTS

Introduction v

Chapter 1   In Case of Emergency 1

Chapter 2   Prepare for the Unexpected 7

Chapter 3   Fire! 17

Chapter 4   Minimizing Fire Damage 23

Chapter 5   Preventing Water Emergencies 35

Chapter 6   Keep a Trickle from Becoming
             a Flood: Minimizing Water Damage 45

Chapter 7   All About Mold 57

Chapter 8   Get Rid of that Mold! 65

Chapter 9   Hurricane Preparedness 75

Chapter 10   Choosing the Right Company 85

Chapter 11   Know Your Insurance 91

Chapter 12   Making a Claim 99

Chapter 13   The Company You Keep 109

Author's Bio 113

INTRODUCTION

How empowering would it be to expertly answer every homeowners' questions on water, fire, or mold emergencies? When all eyes turn to you because your building is smack in the middle of the path of a major hurricane, are you going to nervously hope your ideas work or would you rather take command and prepare your employees and the building with the best methods of handling nature's inevitable onslaught? How much confidence and respect would the residents have in you, and how much confidence would you have in terms of your job security?

My name is Jonathan Fish, and I specialize in fire, water, mold, and natural disaster emergencies. As the owner of National Water Restoration, I'm an expert at preventing, minimizing, and repairing damage to residential and commercial properties. I take worst-case scenarios and change them to best-case scenarios.

I love problem solving and taking on challenges. Just about every day we get a call from a property manager or someone who manages a building, and they are at their wit's end. There are so many quick decisions they need to do, but all they see is their property losing tens or hundreds of thousands of dollars an hour due to something they weren't prepared to handle properly. They look at us to "save the day" and, quite frankly, I love that.

We deal with big issues. When a pipe bursts on the 37th floor of a downtown high-rise in the heart of Miami and 130 units are full of water, that's a huge problem to some. Not me. As I said, that's just a day in life for me, that's a Tuesday. I know, step-by-step, exactly what needs to be done in order of priority to prevent unnecessary damage.

I've dealt with just about every issue a property manager can experience. My company has saved our clients millions of dollars, we've saved peoples' homes, we've saved the jobs of those who called us during a crisis, and we've restored properties back to being fully functional in shorter periods of time than other companies could. I've developed processes and procedures that ensure we send out the right amount of people, equipment, and trucks in the fastest time possible.

I've been told that we are like superheroes. Just like first responders, we are constantly ready for the next emergency. My job is full of action, delegation, crisis prevention, and much more. Emergencies don't adhere to a work schedule; they happen at all hours of the day or night. Phone calls to us are like that bat sign on a cloudy Gotham night.

Part of the reason why my team and I are passionate about what we do is because we've been at the other end of a crisis. We've seen the tears of people whose priceless memorabilia or sentimental objects have been destroyed or rendered useless. We've seen the elderly have to move out to new homes, families uprooted temporarily, and people let go for not knowing how to better handle a crisis situation.

In the case of water, mold, or fire damage, the tenants and sometimes property managers, are usually lost. I don't know about you, but I hate the feeling of being lost. No one likes being lost—very few things frustrate me more. When people are lost, they don't know what to do next and, to make matters worse, they have no idea as to what is covered by insurance and what isn't. Property managers can't answer these questions from emotional tenants:

"Where do I go now?"

"Who's going to pay for my hotel?"

"Who's going to redo my kitchen?"

"What am I liable for?"

"How long do I have to live somewhere else?"

"What do I do now?"

We all fear the unknown. That is why it is important for us to understand different types of policies, what covers water damage, etc. Because of my nine years of experience as a property adjuster, I'm able to answer many questions to those who feel as if they just lost everything. My crew is also knowledgeable in this area. We usually don't give the answer typically given by other technicians, like, *"I don't know sir, I was just called to clean up this here water."*

I never take for granted that some people work their entire lives to live "The American Dream" and own property. It gives me a deep sense of satisfaction that when they felt all hope was lost, I was able to keep them in their homes. I also don't take for granted the trust companies put in us to quickly and efficiently help them through the worst part of owning property.

In just the last 4 years we have serviced over 5,000 properties. In that time, we have climbed the ranks in our industry, and today we are the preferred vendor for some of the largest management companies in the United States. My years of experience in the insurance industry have also given our clients and thousands of homeowners clarity and instruction on their claim process. We take pride in what we do. In fact, one of our employees recently received a Key to the City of Surfside to honor his outstanding service to the city by Surfside's Vice Mayor, Eli Tourgeman.

When accidents do happen, there are policies and procedures you can put in place to significantly mitigate potential damage. Whether you are a property manager, owner, or building maintenance supervisor, it's your business to protect your property. I wrote this book because I wanted to share my knowledge with you so that you can be prepared for any emergency. I hate seeing tens of thousands of dollars and wasted time and effort spent on cleaning up after fires, water leaks, and mold infestations that were preventable.

Each chapter of this book will teach you exactly what you need to know about the most common emergencies that strike residential and business buildings. This book contains everything you need to educate and empower yourself and your staff. Small accidents often turn into large losses when employees don't know how to respond in the first moments of an emergency.

In this book, I share all my secrets, tips, and tricks. I share everything we do and let you know why we do things the way we do them. I break down complex situations to the basics and in a way that is simple to understand. Although I truly enjoy what I do, I know that it's the worst moment for others. If this book just helps one property manager, many families will benefit from it and that's good enough for me.

Keep reading to find out how you can protect your property and prevent or minimize even the worst disasters. The biggest disaster you might make is not reading this book. Prepare yourself to be the best version of yourself when a crisis happens.

It's not a perfect world, but you can handle a disaster perfectly.

CHAPTER ONE

IN CASE OF EMERGENCY

The call came in at 10 a.m. on a Saturday. I wasn't at the office to answer the phone, but Ana, one of my employees, was. The woman on the other end of the phone was frantic.

"You need to get here as fast as possible!"

"Slow down, ma'am. We're here to help," she said. "Let me get your name and the name and address of the building you are talking about." It turned out that she was the property manager of a 12 story high-rise condominium in the heart of Miami, a stylish and luxurious building with 115 units.

"A pipe broke and the entire 6th floor is flooded. There's water everywhere!"

Our trucks and equipment were there by 10:30 a.m., but we found an even bigger problem. Fire trucks surrounded the building and firefighters were scrambling to put out the fire. We came to find out that a pipe had burst at about 8 a.m. on the 6th floor, and now the 6th, 5th, 4th and 3rd floors were flooded, too. That is disastrous for any hotel or condominium. Unfortunately, it wasn't the worst of it.

When the water went through the utility room and got into the meter room, it seeped into the rods that start at the bottom of the building in the electrical room and travelled all the way to the top of the building. The water caused an explosion that tore two of the rods apart, causing a fire and cutting off all electricity to the entire building.

By the time the firefighters had cleared my crew to extract the water, it was a little after 12 p.m. Each floor had 11 units and just about every unit from the 1st to the 6th floor had been compromised with water, some more than others.

The building didn't have any power, so we had to get out our portable generators to extract the water immediately. After extracting the water, we brought out a 300 kW generator to power up the equipment that we needed for the job. Our equipment included approximately 100 dehumidifiers and 300 air-movers placed in locations where they would be most effective. This enabled us to begin the dry-out process.

On the 6th day, the drying process was complete. The time came for us to remove the machines. The project supervisor contacted the property manager and asked her when the electricity would be turned on again. The manager told him that the electricity could be down for at least another month. Not only had the 6th floor lost electricity, but the entire building had no electricity all the way up to the 12th floor. That's when the project supervisor realized the severity of the situation.

It was September, one of the hottest months in South Florida and these apartments had no air-conditioning. The high risk of mold growth was another worrisome factor. The project manager immediately called up the insurance adjuster and informed him of the situation. Together they made a decision to put a dehumidifier and air-scrubber into every single unit of the building, thus mitigating the damages and making sure mold would not grow in the units.

As it was, the families that lived in those 115 units had to leave and find a new place to live, most of whom didn't have insurance. The building was condemned for over 9 months. As of the time this was written, it's still condemned. The truly sad thing about all of this is that these damages could have been avoided!

If someone who worked in the building would have known how to act in a worst-case scenario situation, he or she could have mitigated the problem and saved an incredible amount of money and frustration for the property owners and the families. Unfortunately, when something tragic happens, most people panic. The first instinct we feel as humans at the very moment something disastrous happens is fear for our safety. Not me.

I was born and raised in Israel, more specifically, Jerusalem and the West Bank. As most people are aware, Israel has been a disputed territory for generations. As such, I lived in a constant state of emergency due to the threat of terrorist attacks. I now own a company that specializes in handling water, fire, and mold emergencies, National Water Restoration.

While children in the United States were playing sports, video games, or playing with their toys, I had to take classes at an early age on how to react in times of threats and emergencies. For example, even before I knew how to drive, I learned what to do in case of a drive-by shooting. Do you speed up or break? How do you take control of a car when the driver got hit by a bullet, and you're sitting in the passenger seat? Or, what if there are burning tires on the road—do you drive over the tires, stop, or do a 180 maneuver?

I grew up around emergencies and learning how to best deal with the unexpected, which is partly why I chose a profession that manages crisis situations. It's something that I'm innately good at. Rash, instinctual decisions can very well cost you your life in a place like Israel, but in my profession it can cost property owners hundreds of thousands or millions of dollars. See, I learned never to just run or panic. It was ingrained in me to take two seconds to quickly assess whatever situation I was in and to make a conscious decision, and then act decisively.

If the property manager of the high-rise in Miami would have been prepared and educated, he would have done something other than panic and rush everyone out of the building. More so, the people he rushed out would still be living there, and the building wouldn't be condemned. He probably felt like a hero at the time, but heroes don't panic.

There were two major things that should have been done that weren't. First, as soon as they knew there was a leak, someone should have shut off the water. Secondly, knowing that there would still be a substantial amount of water in the pipes, they needed to empty the pipes. That is what a hero would have done.

That is why I wrote this book, to make sure that you have heroes protecting your properties and not just people that are handy. This book is designed to protect properties everywhere by educating:

- Property Managers
- Chief Engineers
- Building Maintenance Supervisors
- Management Companies
- Insurance Companies
- And anyone whose business it is to protect property from water, fire, or mold.

In just the last year alone, my company, National Water Restoration, serviced over 2,000 properties. We are the preferred vendor of the largest management companies in South Florida. We are equipped with the latest equipment and technology to target all kinds of emergencies. I invested in large trucks to maximize the amount of staff and equipment that we show up with to the job. This ensures we get the job done right the first time.

I understand this business. I understand emergencies, processes, and the importance of quick response. In fact, I have a company policy which states that the faster the technicians show up at the job the bigger the bonus they receive. If they arrive past an acceptable time, they lose this bonus. I'm happy to say. that I'm consistently paying out that bonus. On one occasion, I was invited to speak in front of a group of property managers from First Service Residential. They were having their monthly meeting. When I mentioned the company policy concerning response time, one of the managers raised her hand and said, "I can attest to that. We had an emergency, and I called National Water Restoration. When I picked up my head off the desk, they were right there!"

I also have over 13 years of experience in the insurance industry, so I have in-depth knowledge from that side of the business as well. If you aren't sure how to comply fully with your insurance company, I guarantee you that, sooner or later, it will cost you a lot of money.

The biggest reason for our rapid growth is that we truly specialize in minimizing large losses. Because of that, once someone calls us once, they always call us again the next time and the next. Turn the page to chapter two, and let's get started in proofing your properties so accidents never turn into disasters.

CHAPTER TWO
PREPARE FOR THE UNEXPECTED

They say that two things are certain in this life, death and taxes. The death thing is certain, taxes might depend on who you are and where you live. I think that a truer statement would be this: Two things are certain in this life, death and unexpected bad news. I think that covers everyone regardless of where you live and who you are. Unexpected tragedies occur to everyone. Planes crash, boats sink, and buildings burn or get major water leaks. Just as all planes don't crash and all boats don't sink, not all buildings burn or have major leaks. The truth remains that accidents happen, and there is nothing we can do to avoid them. What we can do is prepare for them.

How can you prepare for something unforeseen?

Too many people whose business it is to protect properties really feel that there is no way to prepare for something unexpected. Unfortunately, the owners of those properties pay a huge price when those people are safeguarding their assets. There are ways to put processes and procedures in place that can help mitigate damage from fire, mold, water leaks, or even a storm. I'm going to mention some, in no particular order.

Understanding the Pipes

Not all buildings are set up the same way. They don't all look alike from the outside, and they certainly don't look alike from the inside. The pipes in a building also differ from building to building.

Many office spaces and condominiums are structured differently when it comes to piping. A high-rise condominium has to have piping in many rooms, such as bathrooms, kitchens, laundry rooms, and air conditioning closets. The newer buildings have sprinkler systems as well. An office building doesn't need pipes going to as many places, maybe just the bathrooms and break rooms. Whatever building you're protecting, make sure you know the layouts of the pipes. To be more specific, know where the connections are in the pipes!

Most pipes break where there are connections. This happens mostly because these pipes are constantly under pressure. After several years, if no one is checking these pipes to ensure they are in proper working order, they will eventually burst. We also see leaks that are the result of poor workmanship on the part of a contractor, such as a plumber, or air conditioner technician who did not glue the pipes together sufficiently, or did so with cheap materials, and the pipes couldn't contain the pressure.

You are going to be amazed as you continue to read this book at how many gallons per minute can gush out of a 6-inch pipe. For now, just know that every minute counts when there is a burst.

If you get a call from a tenant who says there's water all over, and your personnel doesn't know where the connections are, they are going to have a really difficult time locating the leak and shutting off the pipes. So that's the first thing, know your pipes.

Constant Walkabouts

I'm a firm believer that every property manager should take the time to walk the employees around the facility once a month and point out where everything is. It might take 15 or 30 minutes, but there are two great reasons to do this.

1. There is typically high turnover when it comes to maintenance workers, and as a decision maker you want to make sure that all personnel walk through the building so that if someone is new, they know.
2. When there is a high-pressure situation such as a water or fire emergency, if you didn't repeat over and over to the workers where everything is, they most likely won't remember. If you only told your employees 1 time when they started – about 2 years ago – don't expect them to remember where everything is when their hearts are pumping, and it's up to them to stop the outpouring of water that is ruining the building, or a fire that's raging when people are inside the building. Repetition works.

The Shut Off

Every worker should know where the shut off valves are—this is absolutely essential! It is insane for just 1 or 2 people to know how to shut off the water to a million-dollar property. Sadly, this is usually the case. Only the chief engineer knows where everything is. That's crazy! When you are taking your workers on your walkabout, show them how to turn the water on and off.

Tag, You're It

Tag the shut off valves! It may sound simple but most building supervisors or property managers don't put a tag on what is what. In the case of an emergency, someone needs to run into that room and quickly identify which valve is for what and also what direction to turn it in order to shut it off or get it going.

On our website, www.nationalwaterrestoration.com, we have tags that you can get. We actually ship them to you…free! That's right, free. We don't even charge the cost to get them to you. Also, you don't have to be a customer of ours to get them. Make sure that your water or gas valves are clearly marked.

ERP

You should have an Emergency Readiness Program. Have a binder or some sort of book where you physically attach the pictures of the valves and other important things to know during an emergency. Also, next to the picture put a brief description on the location and what it is that each particular valve shuts off. We also have this available for download on our website at www.nationalwaterrestoration.com.

In Case of a Fire

Specific to fires: When a fire does occur, kill the oxygen. For years the understanding was that if there is a fire you should open the doors or windows so that the smoke could escape. Research has proven, especially in high-rises and condominiums, that opening windows or doors actually feeds the fire! It provides the oxygen that the fire needs to sustain itself.

The first thing to do, provided no one is left in the room, is to make sure that the windows are shut and then, when you leave, shut the door behind you. Not doing so is ensuring that the fire will get hotter and spread more quickly.

Divide and Conquer

Teach your team that when an emergency occurs and two people are on duty, they both don't have to see the problem with their own eyes. It's a redundancy of manpower and can cost millions of dollars. Again, make sure that your workers know where the shut off valves are, and make sure that they are tagged properly so even if it's someone's second day on the job, they can turn the correct valve off.

When an emergency happens and there are two people on duty, one person should go inspect it and the other person should head straight to the shut off valves. This way, if it's a serious problem and they are both communicating, the proper valve can be shut off in a timely manner, thus salvaging most of the property and eliminating an incredible amount of headaches in the cleanup and restoration process.

There is a hotel in Boca Raton, Florida that handled a potentially disastrous event perfectly. A sprinkler went off in a room, which of course is the signal for a fire. The chief engineer immediately sent his assistant to investigate the room and make sure the patrons were safe. He headed directly to the shut off room and had his hands on the water valve while his assistant surveyed the scene. The bad news was that there was a fire. The good news was that the fire was only in one section and could be handled. Due to their 'Divide and Conquer' plan, together they were able to get the water shut off very quickly, resulting in only one room being affected. If they had not shut off the water, all the other units would have been soaked needlessly.

Sprinklers

The interesting thing to know about sprinkler systems is that mostly every floor or every other floor has a shut off valve. This way, if there's a fire on the 3rd floor, the sprinklers can be shut off in that specific floor so you don't have to run downstairs and shut off the entire system. Again, during your walkabout, make sure that your staff knows where each shut off point is for the sprinklers on every floor.

The Right Info

One of the biggest and most consistent problems I've seen is that when contractors come in to a property to perform work, they don't have the phone numbers to the front desk or property manager. This is a communication issue that can result in a major loss for a property. The time lost in letting the right people know about the issue has put entire buildings out of commission for weeks and even months. It happens over and over again.

I've been called in to properties and heard story after story about how a contractor tried to hold thousands of gallons of water from pouring out of a pipe as he anxiously thought about who he could call for help. After a few minutes, when he realizes that holding the pipe won't help, he hurriedly runs to take an elevator or run down the stairs. By the time they reach the property manager's office, the water has already severely affected several floors in the building.

When the contractor and/or workers don't have the critically important phone numbers to the front desk and property manager ahead of time, a lot more trouble can occur. Making sure that they have the phone numbers on hand by having them programmed on their cell phone is a simple and extremely effective way to avoid a potentially disastrous situation. All a contractor, who mistakenly broke a pipe, would have to do is call the front desk and inform them on where the pipe broke and have them go shut off the water source. I would also recommend for the property manager to tell the contractor to make sure all of his employees have the same number handy.

Who Do YOU Call?

You just read that every worker should have the number to the front desk or the property manager but...what numbers do the front desk and property managers have for other types of emergencies? Make sure they know who is their current "go-to company" in the event of an emergency. Have them pin it up in their office AND program it in their phones.

What good does it do for someone to quickly call a property manager about an emergency but then that property manager is not in the office and doesn't have the number of the company that can take care of the problem? Make sure that more than one person has that information as well.

Stormy Weather

Storms are slightly different situations but still you can do something to prepare yourself should some unforeseen natural event happen. The first thing you should do when you are notified that a storm is on the way is to put away – indoors – those things that the wind can pick up and use to shatter a window. Things like lawn chairs, toys, etc.

It's important to imagine the conversation with the insurance company if the storm does cause any type of damage. How are you going to convince the insurance company that it was the storm's fault and not because of any negligence on your part? So, go around the property and take pictures of how everything was before the storm. If the storm damages something, you now have tangible evidence of the building before and after the storm.

Take your camera, any camera, and walk through the property and take pictures of just about everything. It might take you a full 40 minutes or an hour, but it will save you time, energy, and a ton of money. Remember, insurance companies will not pay you on something you can't prove. Every little item will be disputed. They will say, "How do we know that wasn't like that before the storm?" So once you brought everything inside, take your camera and click away.

Holy Moldy

The way to protect your property from potential mold issues is to concentrate on your Air Conditioning Unit (A/C). Mold grows when there is too much humidity in a room. When a place has over 60% humidity, that's the perfect atmosphere for mold to take hold. The A/C works like a dehumidifier, it brings the humidity percentage down considerably by essentially taking water out of the air.

Believe it or not, something as simple as changing the filter is one of the best ways to protect a property from mold. When a filter has been used for too long, it restricts airflow. When an A/C doesn't have proper airflow, it doesn't work nearly as well. When you're A/C isn't working well, it allows for pockets of moisture in which mold can grow.

Leaving Town

This is for everyone but more so for those of us that live and/or work in South Florida, where it gets super hot and humid in the extended summer months. For the snow birds and people who leave for more than two weeks at a time, they ask themselves: "Should I turn off my A/C being that no one is going to be here?" Those that opt to turn it off, often come back to a much unhealthier living or workspace than they left.

Here's the rule - Leave the A/C on but shut off the Water Valve!

The A/C

Leave the Air Conditioning unit running even when you are gone. At the highest, set it at 78 degrees. Also, make sure that someone comes to inspect the home or business once a week to do a quick walkthrough to make sure the unit is running properly.

The Water Valve

Shut it off if you are leaving for more than a week. Pipes burst. Due to the industry starting to manufacture plastic fill valves on the pressure pipes of toilets, there has been a rise in pipes breaking behind toilets. Years ago, most companies were making them out of metal and they lasted longer. If you are gone for two weeks and one of these plastic stoppers pops off, imagine how much water damage you are going to wade into when you open the door?

There are many more ways to protect your property before an emergency occurs. I touched on the most important ones in this chapter. As you continue to read the book, you'll see some other valuable tips and tricks. Remember, being prepared can be the difference between an emergency and a nuisance. What would you rather handle?

CHAPTER THREE

FIRE!

The thought of a raging fire burning through your building is a nightmare for anyone. You arrive just as the firetrucks roar up, sirens blaring and lights flashing. The firefighters race past you into the building. Their first concern is to evacuate everyone and search for anyone who might be trapped inside. After that, their job is to put out the fire.

Firefighter Collin Cooper has been fighting fires in Palm Beach and Broward counties for over 10 years. He tells me about a call to a two-million-dollar home in Boca, Florida. The smoke alarm went off. For a smoke alarm alert, only one fire truck is dispatched. They don't speed, and they stop for stoplights. 90% of smoke alarm alerts are false alarms, Cooper says.

But not this time. As they drew closer, Cooper saw smoke billowing into the night sky. The fire had already nearly engulfed the house as the firefighters raced in, searching for survivors. Inside, it was so black with smoke Cooper could barely see. After only a minute, the call came in from command to evacuate. The building was unsafe.

"No, we're okay. We can keep searching!" Cooper said.

"Get out now!" command responded.

Cooper had barely stumbled out of the house when the entire roof collapsed in the blaze. Luckily, there were no fatalities. The family was at a Marlins game.

When people are at home, the first warning is often a smell. The smell of wood smoke from a backyard bonfire can be wonderful, as is the smell of steaks grilling, but the smell of something unnatural burning is different. The stench of plastic, of drywall, of carpet and curtains billowing up in flames is a heady, sickly smell. It inspires fear.

Even the hint of the scent of fire freaks people out. Late last night, I received a call from a man who was certain he smelled smoke. We went over to check it out, and it was nothing. But it isn't always nothing.

Fires are responsible for billions of dollars of damage every year. U.S. fire departments responded to 1.3 million fires in 2014, resulting in over $11.5 billion in property losses. Fires are serious business.

The primary goal is to prevent fires from damaging your properties in the first place, of course. But when fires do happen, you need to have the processes in place to stop the fire as soon as possible and limit the damage.

First Response

The fire alarms are ringing. The stench of smoke stings your eyes and clouds your vision. When there is a fire in a building, people either freeze or panic. Make sure you know beforehand what to do. Make sure your supervisors and property managers all know what to do. All employees should know the address of the building. Make sure the address is clearly marked outside of the building. Go outside, and make sure your address is visible from the street, so that the firefighters don't have to search for the number. In an emergency situation, every second counts.

"Fires are dangerous and unpredictable. No one should go back into a burning building," Cooper warns. The best thing a property manager can do while a fire rages is to clear the way for the firefighters to do their job.

Once the fire trucks show up, your main job as property manager is to clear the way and make sure the entrance is open for the firefighters to do what they are trained to do. Make sure onlookers are not blocking the entrance, the driveway, or the closest fire hydrant. In many counties, firefighters complete yearly walk-throughs of commercial and residential buildings. They know what to do and where to go. Just keep the crowds away and let them do their job.

Once the fire is out, Cooper recommends walking through the entire affected area to make sure the fire really is finished before turning off the alarms or sprinklers. The first thing you want to do is shut off the electrical panel. If it is safe to get into the building, shut it off as soon as you can. Make sure you shut off the sprinklers, too. If you don't manually shut them off, it will keep going for a while and further damage the unit.

Safety After a Fire

We tend to think we are safe once the fire is out. The damage has already been done, so we let our guard down. However, the danger is not over. It is just as important to initiate safety protocols after an emergency as it is to do so beforehand.

Fire-damaged sites are frequently wet following the use of sprinklers and hoses to extinguish the fire. The first item to check after a fire is the power distribution box. Make sure you turn off all breakers at the panel. If only a portion of the building is affected, turn off all breakers providing power to the affected area. This is especially important if water is inside the walls and electrical outlets, or if electrical outlets are located on the floor. It may be necessary to have a licensed electrician do an inspection and check that everything is safe to use.

In a fire, few deaths result from direct contact with flames. The greatest threat comes from the inhalation of the products of combustion, such as carbon dioxide, hydrogen cyanide, hydrogen chloride, and other toxic gases. Smoke is made up of many different gases, many of which are toxic. Once the fire is extinguished, the smoke residue is still extremely harmful to inhale. Make sure that you and any other staff wear dust masks. Gloves, safety goggles, and helmets may also be required, depending on the amount of damage inside the building.

If there is visible exterior damage to a fire-ravaged building, make sure it has passed professional inspections and clearance before you or anyone else enters. If the fire damage is not major, enter carefully. Be aware of broken gas lines, foundation cracks, loose power lines, and holes in the ceiling and floor.

Finding the Source of the Fire

Knowing where fires commonly start is the first step in developing a prevention protocol for residential and commercial buildings.

Fires often start in kitchens. In fact, we do kitchen fires weekly! A mother pours some oil in a pan on the stove. Her baby cries, and she goes to change her baby's diaper. She forgets about the oil, and it catches fire. They aren't necessarily big fires. But sometimes the fire just burns anything it touches. By the time the homeowner turns around, the house is already engulfed in flames.

Don't ever pour water on an oil fire. Oil and water do not mix. When water is poured onto burning oil or grease, the water vaporizes into steam almost instantaneously. As the water changes from a liquid to a gas state, the water expands by up to 1700 times, forcing the fire up and out. If you poured a cup of water into a small beaker of burning oil, the flames instantly surge higher than your head. Instead, you need to suffocate an oil fire with a fire extinguisher or by covering it with a lid.

Lighting and heating malfunctions are also frequent causes of fires. Candles cause fires. Blinds catch fire. Even hoverboards, battery powered scooters, and motored-bicycles were responsible for 16,000 fires in the last year. Cooper describes an increase in fires caused by laptop batteries and computer back-up battery failures. The powerful lithium batteries overheat and rupture, bursting into flame. It was a computer back-up battery that caused the massive roof-collapsing fire at the beginning of this chapter.

Faulty wiring and worn electrical cords cause fires. I've seen a lot of electrical fires. In Aventura, a high end, million-dollar penthouse apartment was empty. A realtor was looking to sell the property and happened to show it that day. A reputable company had installed an expensive, high end fridge. Something happened with faulty wiring, and a part of the fridge caught fire. The sprinkler went off and put the fire out, but the entire eight units underneath the apartment got saturated by water, and smoke filled the entire 4th floor apartment. It caused hundreds of thousands of dollars in damage.

Preventing Fires Before They Start

While all fires can't be averted, an ounce of prevention can save lives and money.

As the property manager, you want to make sure that all lighting, heating, and electric systems are up to date and properly maintained. Check building smoke alarms monthly and change batteries yearly, depending on the brand of alarm.

"The problem with alarms is that they're glitchy, some will go off for no reason," Cooper says. "People get used to just turning them off without checking to see if there is really a problem and, the one time the alarm goes off due to fire, they don't take it seriously and regret it after. So make sure that all alarms work properly, and always check out the area when an alarm goes off."

Make sure that the fire evacuation plan posted for occupants includes instructions to keep windows and doors closed as much as possible. In high rises especially, the wind becomes a serious accelerant. Cooper explains, "Ten years ago, we used to go to a house and break all the windows. Now, we know that can spread the fire." People should keep windows closed and shut doors as they evacuate. "That can save the whole building," Cooper says.

With a solid emergency preparedness plan in place for before, during, and after a fire, the spread of the blaze can be minimized. When the fire is over, however, it is important to act quickly to limit further damage. The majority of property loss is often not from the fire itself, but from its byproducts—smoke, soot, ash, water, and mold. Chapter 4 will explore what you need to know about fire restoration and cleanup.

CHAPTER FOUR
MINIMIZING FIRE DAMAGE

Once the fire is out and the firefighters have finished their work, your own work is just beginning.

You wander through the soot-blackened rooms, the furniture charred and burned, the carpet soggy with water from the sprinklers. The stench of smoke is overwhelming. Slowly, the real panic sets in. What are you going to do? How will this mess ever get cleaned? Is everything ruined?

Don't freak out! Take a deep breath. Then take stock of the situation. Depending on the severity of the fire, not everything will need to be replaced. Professionals can save as much as possible.

Fire restoration is complex. Proper repair depends on many unique factors. In cases more serious than mild fire damage, the best plan of action is to call in a restoration company as soon as possible. Many people don't realize that damage occurs even after the fire is over. Ash is acidic. The longer it is present, the more destruction it causes. Walls, clothing, carpet, and upholstery discolor permanently after only a few days. Glass etches. Metal rusts and corrodes. Wet areas become a haven for mold.

A restoration company like National Water Restoration gets the job done quickly. Most importantly, we get it done right the first time. As a property manager, you don't need to waste needless time and energy or risk making expensive mistakes. The sooner you pick up the phone and hire a professional restoration company, the sooner you get your property back in business.

Protecting Your Assets

You will also want to mitigate losses to your property as soon as possible. If the fire was so extensive that the property must be vacant during repairs, then you need to secure the property. You want to prevent further damage from looting and other issues. Lock the doors. Board up windows. Turn off electricity and water pipes. Insurance companies will also require you to take steps to protect your property.

Make sure you keep thorough photo documentation. Always take pictures for the insurance company before any items are disposed of. You will need proof of every item. So get out your cell phone and snap pictures of everything you see.

Levels of Fire Damage

After you've taken the above steps, the restoration company will come in and complete the cleanup. In order to figure out what level of repair your property is going to need, you'll want to determine how much damage has been done. There are three levels of fire damage: minor, medium, and major damage.

Minor fire damage

With minor damage, your janitorial crew may be able to do the cleanup themselves, as long as they follow the guidelines below. If you are tackling this project yourself, make sure your guys wear rubber gloves, goggles, masks, and other protective clothing. The smoke affects only a few rooms. The amount of smoke residue on the walls is light to moderate.

Have your staff open windows (if the air outside is cooler than the air inside) and get air circulating with fans. Dry wet items as soon as possible with fans and dehumidifiers.

The cleanup process will include dry cleaning or wet cleaning of the ceilings, walls, floors, furniture, and contents of each affected room. Use a coral sponge or other non-water based cleaner to clean porous surfaces. With nonporous surfaces, you can use a mix of detergent and water.

When it comes to curtains and upholstery, make sure you remove the soot before cleaning fabric items. You can hold a vacuum nozzle over the fabric and suck up some of the soot. Don't use vacuum attachment brushes because they can force the soot further into the fibers.

Once you've removed soot from the carpets, cover them with plastic or cardboard to keep them from becoming re-contaminated. Make sure you deodorize clothes, carpets, and draperies before cleaning, or you may not be able to get the smoke odor out. Most household deodorizer sprays don't work.

You can remove minor smoke film from washable surfaces with a solution of heavy-duty cleaner or degreaser with a small amount of deodorizer.

To clean windows covered in soot, use one part rubbing alcohol to five parts traditional window cleaner.

Repaint areas as needed. With minor cases like this, very few items will need to be replaced, and most items can be cleaned onsite if done properly.

Medium Fire Damage

With medium damage, there is a lot more smoke residue. There will be heat damage to drywall, cabinets, and personal property. The odor of smoke will be very noticeable. If your staff is doing the cleanup, it will take a lot more heavy-duty work to get the property back in working order. You'll need to repaint larger areas of walls and ceilings and sometimes replace parts of them. Many items will be beyond saving, and you'll have to trash them. You may need to replace or refinish the flooring.

Because the smoke is so pervasive, the affected areas may require several deodorizing treatments to remove the stench. The insulation in the ceiling will have to be removed and replaced. Air conditioning ductwork may need to be cleaned or replaced.

Major Fire Damage

Don't try to handle major fire damage yourself. Call in a professional restoration company immediately. In major cases, heat, fire, and smoke have caused extreme damage to the property. Heavy smoke residue will cover most areas of the building. The smoke odor permeates everything. The structure and framing may be damaged and may need to be completely replaced. Personal property needs to be replaced.

Emergency services are also needed. The electricity will be turned off to avoid another fire. The property must be vacated and boarded up. Restoration and clean up will involve major cleaning of the structure. All portable equipment, furniture, and other materials will require removal for off-site cleaning. In order to get the smell out, many different methods, such as encapsulating, deodorizing, and sonic cleaning will need to be used.

The structure may be damaged to the point that it cannot be cleaned and restored. In that case, reconstruction is required.

Determine What Burned

The restoration company needs to know what caused the fire. We want to know what burned. Everything that burns releases a different type of chemical. Some chemicals are harder to clean and are more toxic.

If you burn a piece of paper, the ashes fall on the table. You can wipe it with your hand because it's wood or synthetic. If you burn a piece of chicken with a lighter, the chicken has grease, which is harder to clean. If you touch it, then try to wipe it off with your hands, you'll only make it worse by smudging it. Once we know what exactly burned, we know what method to use for the cleaning.

This is another reason why professionals need to conduct the restoration. Let us handle these things. We understand the differences and unique requirements for each type of fire.

Types of Soot

Residue that is left behind on walls and furniture is called soot. Not all soot residue is the same, and some types of soot are easier to clean than others. First, we always identify the type of residue and the material the residue affects, and then we capture the residue in dry particulate form or in a solution. Finally, we remove the residue and properly dispose of it.

Dry smoke residue

Burning wood, paper, wool, cotton, and natural fibers causes something called dry smoke. These materials tend to produce a dry, powdery smell with no smear residue. This is usually the easiest soot to clean. You can easily wipe it down with a coral sponge.

Wet smoke residue

Wet smoke is caused by burning material such as plastic, rubber, and foam. This type tends to produce wet and easily smeared residue.

Protein smoke residue

This type of residue is mostly found in kitchen fires involving burning meats, such as fish or poultry. These materials usually leave a greasy, yellow residue, causing very little paint discoloration on your cabinets' surfaces. Many times you don't even notice the residue. But it's a very hard resident—a beast—and you need to use special degreasers to get it off.

Fuel or oil smoke residue

This occurs mostly in the Northeast. The furnace puffs back or one of the oil burners suddenly catches on fire. This is the toughest soot to clean up and requires special solutions and chemicals.

Restoring fire-damaged structures

There are several ways we attempt structural cleaning. Before cleaning the structure, we determine the appropriate cleaning method, i.e. washable versus non-washable. Washable materials can be wet-cleaned, where applying a solution-cleaning product to the material will not damage the material. With non-washable materials, or materials that cannot be wet, applying liquids to the material may damage it. So, the material must be cleaned using a dry method.

Factors affecting cleaning

The age of the surface affects how easy it will be to clean. Generally, the older the surface, the harder it is to clean. The type of surface also plays a big role in cleaning. Smoke sinks into porous surfaces, allowing it to penetrate further. Porous surfaces are much more difficult to clean. Nonporous surfaces, such as plastic, glass, and enamel paint, are easier to clean than surfaces that are porous like wallpaper or wood.

Getting Rid of that Smoke Smell

If you've ever tried to get that unpleasant smoke smell out of a jacket or the used car you just bought, you know how tenacious it can be. You wash, scrub, and clean again and again, yet the stink remains.

There is no instrument that is able to detect odor except for your nose. And yet, the smell that smoke leaves behind can be a real problem. The size of a smoke particle is .004 micros, which is difficult for the human eye to see without a microscope. These particles get inside walls, cabinets, behind baseboards, and beneath carpets, making them almost impossible to clean without a professional.

There are two types of odors to deal with after a fire: real odor and imaginary odor.

Real Odor

Real odor is the smell caused by a real substance. The odor molecules interact with our nerve cells in our nose. Our nerves send the message to our brain, which interprets the smell. And that post-fire smell is especially pungent.

Luckily, professional restoration companies can successfully rid your property of that smoke stench. And you don't have to gut an entire apartment. Professionals use special coral sponges. We get into every single nook and cranny by hand. For bigger jobs, such as commercial warehouses, we bring in heavy-duty tools.

We had a job in Mid-Town at a fabric distribution center. The landlord wheeled an old trailer into his storage area, and somehow the wheel caught on fire, starting a major blaze. This was a 38,000 square feet fabric distribution center, with rolls and rolls and rolls of fabric. They had a major smoke out, and we had to clean everything, tag everything, and fix the actual structure. The procedure we use is called soda blasting – it's a machine compressor that spouts out soda. It is a quick and effective tool for removing soot and cleaning charred building materials. As an added benefit, the baking soda helps neutralize the smoke odor.

We use sand blasting with more difficult cases. Another way to eliminate order is by fogging, which requires using a machine and special solutions or chemicals that create a cloud similar to the smoke fire. This cloud solution emulates the smoke cloud and attaches itself to the soot, removing the smell. Newer technology is also applied, such as a hydroxyl generator, and that also kills the odor.

The way we clean smoke odor is by removing the odor source, such as soot. Then we clean the surface and re-create the conditions that caused the odor penetration. We can create the same conditions that caused the odor by using either a thermal fogger or ozone machine.

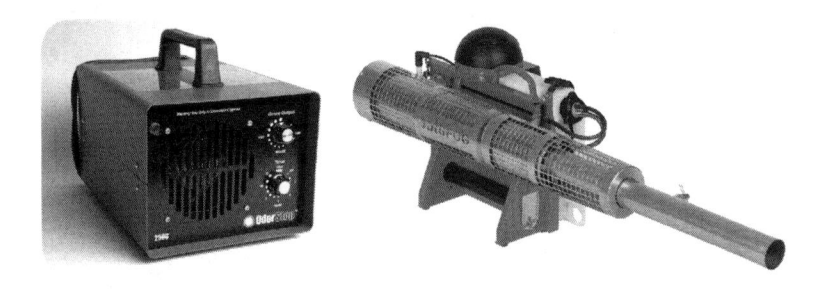

These machines basically spread a cloud of the deodorizer that penetrates into the same areas that the smoke has gone into. The deodorizer attaches itself to the smoke and basically cancels out the odor. Afterward, we seal the surfaces that were exposed.

Imaginary Odors

Sometimes people think they smell something because of the circumstances, not because there is actually an odor present. We call this "heightened-awareness odor," because if a person thinks that they should smell something, then they will smell something even though other people don't. It's all in their head. This is a major problem when it comes to fire and mold.

Specialty Cleanup Services

Specialty items such as electronics, clothing, furniture, and art are often sent out to specialty restoration cleaning services. They use a method of dry cleaning or ultrasonic cleaning.

Electronics

With fire or any type of damage, electronics should always be cleaned. There are special cleaning centers that utilize an ultrasonic cleaning process. They can clean and dry the electronics without damaging them. If homeowners have affected computers, they should ask the insurance adjuster to recommend one of these companies. The technology is out there that can clean these devices.

Artwork

When cleaning artwork, there are two types of art—valuable and less expensive. Less expensive art does not warrant the costly, specialized service of a restorer. The restorer can attempt to clean the artwork after explaining to the customer that the cleaning process may affect the visible appearance of the item.

Valuable art, however, requires the skill of a trained restorer. We will usually subcontract a fine art restoration to do the restoring. It is important that during the restoration process, the restorer, property manager, and insurance adjuster work hand-in-hand together to ensure that the claim process is smooth and all details are accounted for.

Don't Forget the Ceiling

We all know that when there is fire and smoke, we need to stay low. The reason for that is that heat rises. Therefore, the smoke continues upward until it is stopped by the ceiling. The greatest concentration of smoke immediately after the fire will be in the ceiling. As the upper portion of a room fills up, the smoke moves into another room, and then another. The smoke goes into the vents and right into the air-conditioning system.

The ductwork of the air-conditioning system can spread smoke throughout the structure. The restorer may not need to clean the A/C system in every case of fire damage, but they do need to inspect the system and test for smoke. Air-conditioning cleaning is usually needed in moderate and heavy smoke damage situations. If contaminated ducts are not cleaned, they can distribute smoke back into the structure when the air conditioner is turned on again.

We generally use two machines to clean ducts. One is the air scrubber. This is used to remove the particulates from the air and clean the air. The second tool is an electrical brush that is used to scrub the ductwork, and the loose soot gets sucked into the air scrubber.

The work required after a fire can seem overwhelming. But a restoration company eases the burden considerably. We have the expertise and the experience to handle even the biggest fire disasters. We know what we're doing, and we will bring your property back to its original condition. Restoration companies like National Water Restoration respond to all kinds of disasters, not just fire. In chapter five, we will explore ways to protect your property from water-related emergencies.

CHAPTER FIVE
PREVENTING WATER EMERGENCIES

The tenant of a unit on the 20th floor of a high-rise apartment in Fort Lauderdale lit a candle one evening. At nine o'clock at night, she left her apartment to drive to the west coast of Florida. She left the candle burning. Somehow, the candle flame caught the sofa on fire. Soon, the living room was in flames.

A minute later, the sprinkler sensor registered heat. Not only did the sprinkler in the unit switch on, but when the smoke detectors detected the smoke from the fire, every sprinkler on the 20th floor turned on as well. Because there was an actual fire, property manager, Carol Bens couldn't turn off the sprinklers until the firefighters arrived.

"It was a monster," says Bens. Six units were affected on every single floor down to the lobby. The water leaked right down through the floor and created a lot of damage.

Sometimes there isn't much you can do to prevent a water emergency. Accidents happen. But you can be smart. Educating yourself, your staff, and your tenants about how water damage happens and what to do in the event of a water emergency is an important preventative step.

Where Water Comes From

There are dozens of places where water can leak in your property, including toilets, washing machines, dishwashers, water heaters, air-conditioning systems, fridge icemakers, and of course, sprinklers and pipes. According to the Environmental Protection Agency, 13.7% of all water used residentially can be attributed to plumbing leaks.

It only takes a few minutes for water to do serious damage. Time is absolutely of the essence when 700 gallons of water is gushing out of a pipe every single minute. To give you a sense of scope, notice these common pipe sizes and how much water these larger pipes can pump out:

A half inch pipe= up to 21 gallons per minute
A one-inch pipe= up to 58 gallons per minute
A two-inch pipe= up to 200 gallons per minute
A three-inch pipe = up 425 gallons per minute
A four-inch pipe =up to 700 gallons per minute
A five-inch pipe= up to 1100 gallons per minute
A six-inch pipe = up to 1700 gallons per minute
An eight-inch pipe= up to 2800 gallons per minute

That's a lot of water! The average bathtub holds 45 gallons. An average six-foot deep in-ground pool contains just under 11,000 gallons. An eight-inch pipe at its max is pumping a pool into your property every four minutes. Think about that for a second.

An emergency preparedness plan that can cut your response time by 15 to 20 minutes or more is going to save thousands of dollars in water damage.

Know Your Pipes

Every type of building is unique, whether it's condominiums, offices, hotels, or hospitals. Condominium buildings will have pipes going to every single unit, with supply lines to water heaters, fridge water dispensers, sinks, toilets, dishwashers, showers, and sprinkler systems. Office buildings will have sprinkler systems throughout, as well as pipes leading to bathrooms and air conditioners. It's important for personnel to know the layout of your individual building.

Know Your Sprinklers

Your building's sprinkler system set up begins as a six or eight-inch pipe that branches out throughout the building like a structure of veins or arteries. The sprinkler pipe pulls its water directly from the city. There's no big tank or reservoir, so the water will only stop if the pipe valve is shut off. Also, the water coming out of the sprinkler pipes is usually dirty. Sometimes it even has grease in it, because the pipes are so seldom used.

In the utility room, there's a pump that pushes the water into the pipes. Right after the pump, there's a shut off valve. There are also shut off valves on every floor. Usually, these will be in the stairwells.

There are sprinklers in every room and hallway. Each sprinkler head has a little glass bulb that breaks when heated or struck, which activates the water flow.

The amount of water that comes out of the sprinkler depends on the size of the building, but on average it is between 20 and 40 gallons per minute. The bigger the building, the bigger the pipes and pump. The purpose of these sprinkler systems is to put out fires, so they push out a lot of water.

Shutting Off the Sprinkler System

Building management is allowed to shut off the sprinkler system once they know there is not a fire. They are also allowed to silence the alarm system, but not shut it off. That needs to be done by the fire department. The fire department can see exactly where the alarm went off and take the necessary steps to secure the property before resetting the alarm.

The fire alarm warns people of a fire, and the sprinkler system puts the fire out. As soon as that bulb breaks, two to three dozen gallons per minute are coming out of that pipe. Like the example of the chief engineer in the beginning of this book, smart moves can save a tremendous amount of damage. When the engineer heard there was a sprinkler pop in his building, he immediately ran downstairs to the pump room while one of his maintenance guys ran up to check out the sprinkler. As soon as the engineer got the call that there was no fire, the engineer shut off the pump. The damage was isolated to a single room.

Twenty minutes of preparation and a knowledgeable staff can prevent major damage to your property.

Educate Your Staff

One of the most important things you can do is to make sure every member of your staff knows where all the shut off valves are for all the pipes running through your building. This includes the engineering crew, the maintenance crew, janitorial, and security.

Whoever is on duty needs to know where shut off valves are and how to shut them off. They need to know power shut offs, valve and sprinkler shut offs, and valve shut offs to each unit. They should know the valve for the entire building and every floor.

It's better to shut off the valve at the floor instead of the whole building because often the water will continue to flow until the pipes are empty. And remember, these are big pipes!

Tagging pipes and shut off valves for water, electric, and gas is one of the best preventative measures you can take.

These identifying tags are free on my website, at nationalwaterrestoration.com. Even though city inspectors come out annually to make sure pipes and valves are labeled, that doesn't mean your staff knows how to read the tags correctly or find the right valve quickly. Our tags are easy to read and identify in an emergency situation.

In addition to tagging each shut off valve, take a few minutes to tour the building with your staff every month or so. Point out important locations on each floor and in the utility room. Practice drills can be very helpful as well. In an emergency situation, if a staff member is told to "run down to the utility room and turn the red valve," they may go down but not know which direction to turn the valve. It's a large valve; it's hard to turn. It can also get stuck. He gets confused, and confusion costs valuable seconds.

Every staff member needs to feel comfortable responding to an emergency situation. Most valves are not difficult to turn off. It's mostly a matter of seeing the valves in person and knowing where they are, essentially being prepared. That's what makes a difference in an emergency.

Emergency Readiness Folder

I also recommend an emergency readiness folder. This folder contains pictures of all shut off valves, where they are located, and what they are for. The folder should also contain the names of every contractor the building uses.

On Saturday morning, when there's a leak on the 8th floor and you're 40 minutes away, the security guard will reference the book. He knows what valve to shut off and who to call.

I provide an emergency readiness folder template on my website free of charge. Download the template, add in your own information and pictures, and print it out. You're good to go.

The Importance of a Phone Number

Just as it's important for your crew to have every contractor's number, it's equally important that every contractor who enters your building has the number of the front desk and property management office programmed into his phone. He needs to know who to call immediately, so that management can send someone to fix the problem.

For example, say a painting contractor is painting several rooms on the 5th floor. While he's painting, he accidentally pops a sprinkler. He grabs the sprinkler and tries to stop the water, but of course he can't. Now he has to run through the building to find the front desk. In the 15 minutes it takes him to get downstairs, three floors have filled with water.

This scenario happens a lot. One of the top causes of water damage is contractors accidentally popping pipes. Once, we had a situation where an A/C contractor twisted a pipe too hard, and it broke. He tried to stop the water flow himself, but he couldn't do it. He finally climbed down his ladder, but he couldn't remember where the elevator was. By the time he got downstairs, it was a disaster. The pipe broke on the 7th floor, but within minutes, 3 floors had water damage. By the time we arrived, the 7th floor looked like a swimming pool, like a shining river of water 3 inches deep. We got our extraction machines, and in 20 minutes the water was completely gone.

In both of the above situations, if the contractor had the front desk number programmed into his phone, the crisis would have been averted.

Educate Your Tenants

SPRINKLERS

Many people don't understand how sensitive a sprinkler head is. People will use it as a hanger and hang clothes on it, especially in hotels. Sometimes they accidentally bump into it, and even a small amount of pressure can pop the bulb.

Some hotels actually place a tag on the wall next to the sprinklers warning guests not to hang clothes on it. It's a good idea to put little stickers under sprinkler heads instructing people not to tamper with it.

PREPPING FOR VACATION

Tenants and homeowners need to be instructed to always shut off the water before leaving on a trip. Many fill valves are now being made of plastic instead of metal. They aren't made to last for very long. After a certain number of years, they pop. You leave your apartment for the summer, and 3 months in, the pressure pipes burst behind the toilet.

Managers should instruct tenants on how and where to shut off the water pipes. Or, management can send someone to shut it off before the homeowner leaves.

Tenants should also make sure windows are closed, especially in high-rise apartments and condominiums where wind-driven rain will blow water into the unit.

REPORTING WATER DAMAGE

Some people don't know what the beginning stages of water damage looks like. Others may not realize the importance of reporting related incidents immediately. Educate your tenants and make sure they have the correct numbers to call in case of an emergency.

When Disaster Strikes

Now that you've taken the steps to avert preventable water emergencies, developed your emergency preparedness folder, and trained your staff, you are well prepared in the event that a water emergency does happen. And if it does, chapter six will guide you through the process of minimizing the damage so that you can get your property back into tip-top shape as soon as possible.

CHAPTER SIX
KEEP A TRICKLE FROM BECOMING A FLOOD: MINIMIZING WATER DAMAGE

The immediate crisis is over. The burst pipe is shut. You've managed the emergency with the least amount of destruction possible. Now, it's time to get rid of the water, clean up, and restore your property to full working order.

In situations with limited flooding, your maintenance crew may be able to properly clean up on their own. In more extensive cases, a professional water restoration company should come in as soon as possible. A company that knows what they're doing can restore more than you might think, which saves you time, money, and hassle. Your goal now is to prevent further damage from standing water and mold growth.

Types of Water Damage

The type of water determines whether special care needs to be taken during clean up and restoration. It's important to identify the source of the water damage to assess whether the water is contaminated. Gray and black water are not the actual color of the water, but they act as a guideline for the level of contaminates in the water.

The 3 categories of water are:

CLEAN WATER

Water from burst pressure pipes, such as water filters and water supply lines. This is the easiest to clean up since most of the time all that is needed is a proper dry out. Still, clean water needs to be removed quickly to prevent mold. Clean water can become gray if it sits for 48 hours.

GRAY WATER

Gray water may contain chemical or bacterial contaminants. This is water from an overflowing toilet, shower, dishwasher, or a washing machine—it is "used" water. Technicians will determine the proper course of the restoration depending on the cleanliness of the water. In many cases, sterilization and disinfectants are sufficient fo r completing the job. Anyone working on the property should wear gloves. After 48 hours, gray water is considered black water.

BLACK WATER

Black water is hazardous. This type of water includes flooding from natural disasters or sewage back-ups and pipe overflows. Black water can contain toxic elements like pesticides. All raw sewage contains microbes such as bacteria, fungi, and viruses. Do not attempt any kind of black water cleanup on your own. Hire a professional company to restore the water damage. Masks, gloves, and other precautions will be taken to prevent infection and illness.

With black water, take considerable care to inspect and test the property to make sure the health hazard has been completely removed before allowing anyone back into the affected area.

In cases of black water, the majority of items will need to be thrown away. Carpeting needs to be ripped up, drywall removed, and drapes and upholstery discarded.

Luckily, most water emergencies are not black water. With clean water and sometimes gray water cases, as long as the property is dried within 48 hours, further problems are unlikely. The good news is that your maintenance crew or a professional water restoration company can salvage most of your property, including the drywall.

Dry Out or Cut Out

Is it better to just cut out the wet drywall and replace it with new drywall, or is it better to dry it in place?

Cutting out is the physical removal of wet materials that includes insulation, carpeting, paneling, drywall, and other porous building materials. In North America, drywall is the most common interior wall and ceiling material. Normally it is composed of paper on both exterior surfaces, which is laminated to a gypsum core. Drywall is easily damaged while wet, since it loses much of its strength and stiffness. If it doesn't remain wet for extended periods, drywall normally regains its original strength as it dries.

While there are situations where cutting out water-damaged material is needed, such as with black water flooding, usually the best option is drying it out. Tearing out drywall is a huge headache. It is expensive, messy, and takes time.

With drying out drywall, there are no required permits. It is more convenient, cost efficient, and faster. The unit or business is still habitable. Drywall dries out in 3 to 5 days, while construction can take weeks.

Property managers and owners should feel 100% comfortable with drying out drywall. Today, with the proper technology and equipment, the drying process is guaranteed to be 100% efficient and will restore your property to pre-loss condition.

Dry out also limits your liability. The less workers and the less hazardous materials that you deal with, the less chance of anything going wrong. It is also guaranteed to be insurance approved, because insurance companies want to minimize damage and save money, too.

Dry out is also an advantage in recovery time, cost, convenience, and liability. It's the industry standard. While cutting out may be guaranteed, the industry has so perfected the dry out process that insurance companies will not agree to cut out unless absolutely necessary.

NATIONAL WATER RESTORATION
EXCELLENCE • INTEGRITY • RELIABILITY

CASE STUDY

KEEP A TRICKLE FROM BECOMING A FLOOD: MINIMIZING WATER DAMAGE

	Dry-out	Cut-Out
Emergency Call	$150	$150
Water Extraction	$220	$220
Dehumidification	$1,325	$320
Air Movers	$860	$215
Kitcken Cabinets	320 (Toe Kick)	$1325 (Detach & Reset)
Granite Countertops	$0	$2300 (Break Risk)
Content Removal	$95	$95
Demolition & Disposal	$0	$1,950
Drywall, Base & Paint	$1,400	$6,500
Plumbing & Electrical	$0	$950
Permits	$0	Unknown
Hotel Stay	$700	$2,100
Grand Total	**$5,070**	**$16,120**
Turnaround Time	6 days	14-21 Days + Material Time

*This is an example, every case is different.

Drying Drywall

Drywall does not lose its integrity if you dry it. In fact, studies show drywall that has been wet and then dried is even stronger. There are several fairly simple steps you can take to properly dry drywall in small flooding situations.

Say you have water from the ceiling that leaks down the entire wall from ceiling to floor. All you really need to do is cut the top of the baseboards with a blade so it doesn't take off the paint, then pop off the baseboards. You drill a few ¾ inch holes on the bottom and top of the wall. Point a fan at the bottom holes to move air through the area. 3 to 5 days later, the wall is dry. Just fill in the holes, put baseboard back on, repaint, and you're done. You'd never know you had a flood.

Sometimes, though, there is hidden damage. When water gets under baseboards, it saturates the insulation. You will get mold growth. If you see that it went under the baseboards, you need to take off the baseboards and check to see that the insulation is dry.

If the water damage is extensive, or there is more damage than you thought, the best thing to do is to call in a professional restoration company as soon as possible.

The Drying Process

A water-damaged property needs to be thoroughly dried. We must remove the moisture from every material in an effort to prevent permanent and secondary damage.

When we enter a water-damaged property, the first thing we do is use an extraction machine to suck out the standing water.

Then we deal with the water that's trapped in the carpet or in the walls. We use an air mover to get the water molecules out of the wall and into the air, and then we can capture the water in the air with a dehumidifier.

The goal is to extract, evaporate, dehumidify, and control the temperature. We want to get the affected property as equally dry as the rest of the unaffected area.

In large losses, we use commercial dehumidifiers known as desiccant dehumidifiers. These types of dehumidifiers are able to remove large amounts of moisture. Desiccant dehumidifiers are best for warehouses and big, open spaces.

What's With Humidity?

You've heard the phrase, "It's not the heat, it's the humidity." Well, humidity is also a culprit in water damage.

Humidity refers to the amount of water vapor in the air. The more molecules in the air, the more humidity we feel. There's always a certain amount of humidity because water is constantly evaporating, especially in hot environments like South Florida. The temperature in the air causes water to evaporate, or be drawn up into the air.

An hour after it rains, if it is hot, the water will be gone. However, if you took a plastic tablecloth and covered the wet ground, the water would not disappear. The water evaporates, but it cannot escape from beneath the plastic, so it falls back to the ground in water droplets. Sealed bottles of water or Coke do not dry up because the molecules cannot escape.

The same idea happens in the case of water damage. Immediately after a water leak, you will feel a lot of humidity. The water seeks drier air to escape to and begins evaporating. The hotter the temperature in the room, the faster the evaporation. The faster the evaporation, the more molecules in the air, causing high humidity.

If the molecules are not captured and removed, they will fall right back down on furniture or walls or the floor. We call that secondary damage. It can actually damage new property that was not affected by the initial water emergency. To prevent further damage, you need to get the molecules out of the property as soon as possible.

The goal is to lower the humidity in the damaged room to the same level as the unaffected spaces. Professional companies have tools to accurately test the amount of water in an area. Every day we monitor how much the humidity has dropped. When it is the same as the unaffected area, we know it's dry.

Air Movers Versus Dehumidifiers

We use air movers for ventilating areas that are damp or wet. The ventilation speeds up the evaporation of moisture and transfers the moisture from the material into the air. Air movers don't dry, but they help the evaporation process. The air movers can move the water molecules around, but they can't capture the molecules. So a fan alone will not reduce the humidity in the damaged area.

Often, a janitorial crew will put fans in a water-damaged area to try and dry it out themselves. The walls will feel dry and seem fine. But they aren't. The evaporated water is still in the air in the room. It has nowhere to go, so it condenses back into water. Where does it go? You guessed it: it goes right back into the damaged wall or carpet.

This is where the dehumidifier comes in. Dehumidifiers remove excess moisture in the air by converting water vapor into liquid form so it can be easily removed. Dehumidifiers process the air, but the water needs to be in the air in order to process it. You need both the air movers to move the molecules into the air, and the dehumidifier to capture them.

Using an air mover without a dehumidifier or a dehumidifier without an air mover will not be effective. They must work together to dry properly. Also, if you use a dehumidifier and air mover without first removing the excess water, it can take too long to dry, causing permanent damage and mold.

Windows Open or Shut?

Do you open windows after water damage or keep them shut? The answer is, it depends. If the air outside is less humid than inside, then open the windows. The dry air will draw out the humid air in the room.

If it's the opposite, if it's a sweltering summer day, keep the windows closed. If you don't, you're bringing in air that is even more moist. Opening the windows in this situation can speed up mold formation.

Although sometimes you can tell by the feel of your skin, we use a special tool to test the humidity outside versus inside.

Tools of the Trade

It is extremely important to use the right tools. Make sure your water restoration company is using the proper equipment to dry your property effectively.

- Thermo-hydrometer. We use this to test the air outside the property versus the air in the room. This will immediately tell us if we should keep the windows closed or open.

- Thermo-imaging or infrared camera. Sometimes we don't know exactly what's wet. Drywall can look and feel dry, but the inside is still moist. We'll use the thermo-imaging camera to see which areas are wet. The cool, wet areas look blue.

- Air injectors. This tool injects air behind the drywall to increase airflow and push the water molecules out of the wall.

- Air movers. These get the water molecules out of the drywall, carpet, or other materials and into the air.

- Dehumidifiers. Dehumidifiers capture the water in vapor form and transform it into a liquid.

- Penetrating and non-penetrating moisture meter to accurately test the humidity. The only time I would recommend using only these moisture meters is in a case like a construction zone where you cannot stabilize the environment properly because you have workers walking in and out and opening doors and windows all the time. Then I would check section by section with a moisture meter. Otherwise, I would take the readings with the thermal hydrometer as well.

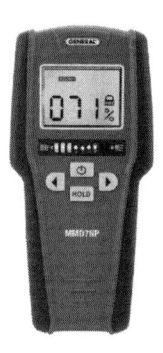

For example, we had a building that was being completely renovated, and they had a sprinkler pop on the 4th floor that flooded 3 floors of the construction zone and a downstairs restaurant. The construction supervisors made it clear they would not stop the renovation of the building as it was too costly. So we made the decision to have our drying goals met by checking section by section with moisture meters.

When water damage isn't caught quickly enough, mold develops. Mold can start growing in damp areas in as little as 24-48 hours. Mold can be a scary concept because it is often hidden in places we don't see. Everyone has heard stories of toxic mold making people sick.

Professional restoration companies like National Water Restoration work hard to fix mold problems. In chapters seven and eight, we'll explore exactly what causes mold, how to prevent it, and how to get rid of it once and for all.

CHAPTER SEVEN
ALL ABOUT MOLD

One Friday morning, I got a call from an old apartment building in West Palm Beach. A pipe had burst, and there was a flood of water in the utility room 8 inches deep. We came in and pumped the water out using submersible pumps.

Most of the walls were concrete and dried quickly, but there were a couple of walls of drywall. I spoke with the property manager and recommended that we put some dehumidifiers and air movers in the area to dry them up, but the property manager said no. He didn't want to spend the extra money.

Two months later, the property manager called us back in desperation. There was mold everywhere. The drywall was in the same room as the air conditioner handler. Mold colonies infested the damp drywall and transferred into the air conditioner. The mold traveled through all the air conditioning ducts in the hallways of the entire building. The mold was so bad, you could see it all over the A/C ducts and the air vents.

Of course, the property manager could have prevented the entire situation if he'd taken the steps to properly dry out the wet area. He thought small scale—save a few bucks now—instead of large scale—a little bit of money will save tens of thousands of dollars later. And, he didn't really understand the dangers of mold. He didn't realize how quickly it grows and spreads.

There seems to be a lot of mystery surrounding the idea of mold, but there doesn't need to be. Mold, like anything else, can be minimized and even prevented with the right procedures and processes in place.

What Exactly is Mold?

Mold is a type of fungus that decomposes organic matter. It is a multi-celled organism with tubular branches called mycelium, which appears like very fine, fuzzy threads. Mold colonies often form spherical or round shapes.

Mold spreads through tiny spores in the air and through the extension of hyphae, which are like tiny root hairs. Spores float through air or water and land on new areas, rapidly spreading mold if the conditions are right. Mold spores are extremely small, about .003 microns, so you can't really even see mold until it settles and colonizes. A small colony can grow to cover over 100 square feet.

"Mold is ubiquitous," explains Richard M., a mold assessor in the industry for over 30 years. "It's everywhere." Mold spores are in the air both outside and inside.

The problem happens when mold spores find a damp, tasty spot to dig in and grow. "The mold is there to begin with," Richard M. says. "The water accelerates the growth. It accelerates what is already present in the environment."

Mold requires a source of nutrition and a source of water. Most types of mold also need oxygen. Mold grows on organic material such as wood, paper, dust, food particles, fabric, carpet, and gypsum in drywall.

Mold also grows quickly in dark, stagnant areas. It prefers warm temperatures, damp materials, and high humidity.

Is Mold Dangerous?

There are over 1000 different types of mold in the United States. Some types of mold are not toxic unless there is a large amount in a small area. Other types of mold, such as *Stachybotrys Chartarum*, aka black mold, is toxic even in small amounts. However, even black mold has not been proven toxic to breathe. You would need to eat it in order to experience symptoms of toxicity. However, it's important to note that any type of mold can cause health problems in certain people if there is enough of it.

According the CDC, certain people are more sensitive to health effects from mold. People with mold allergies, chronic illnesses, immune-compromised individuals, and young children are more susceptible. For these people, mold can cause nasal stuffiness, throat irritation, coughing, wheezing, eye irritation, rashes, headaches, upper respiratory infections, asthma, and even lung infections.

How Can I Tell if I Have Mold?

Although mold is everywhere, in most cases the mold spores are not activated because there is nothing for them to feed on. When there is water and damp areas, then the mold spores that are already present become active and grow and multiply.

The most important thing you want to do is be observant, suggests Richard M. "Observe for moisture, staining, and dampness. If you see water stains, that indicates there is or was a problem." If you walk into a unit or a room, and the air is musty, or if there is a strong moldy smell, then you know you've got a problem. Mold emits a smell when it is viable and actively reproducing. If you can smell it, it's there.

That being said, it can be hard to recognize the mold smell if you aren't familiar with it. There are many reasons an apartment might smell that have nothing to do with mold. I get a lot of calls where the property manager tells me one of his tenants smells something, or their kid is coughing a lot, and they're worried about mold.

Sometimes it's just in their head. They're worried, so they want a test to make sure there's no mold. I can come in with my infrared camera and moisture meter and test to see if anything is wet. Half of the testing Richard M. does is for peace of mind. But people want to know for sure, and that's okay.

"The first thing I do is that I walk in, and I smell the place," he says. "The next step is, I'll do a moisture survey using a thermo-hydrometer (see chapter 6). If there's no elevated moisture and there's no smell, I'm thinking there's probably not a problem."

Of course, sometimes there is a problem. And sometimes you can see the mold. Good spots to look for mold include dark, wet places: bathrooms, closets, laundry rooms, around windows, and around A/C units.

Sometimes mold is hidden. According to the EPA, common hiding spots include the back side of drywall, wallpaper, or wall paneling, the top of ceiling tiles, the underside of carpets and pads, condensation drain pans inside air handler units, and roof materials above ceiling tiles due to roof leaks.

Testing For Mold

If you see or smell mold, you'll need to get it tested. If tenants are complaining of coughing and/or a moldy smell, have someone check it out.

There are a few different types of tests. There is an air test, which uses cassette samplers that suck air through a disk and force spores onto a sticky collection media.

Depending on the brand, a certain number of liters of air should run through the cassette tester, for example, 150 liters of air in 10 minutes or 75 liters of air in 5 minutes. The research recommends 15 liters of air every minute for 10 minutes, says Richard M.

It is important to conduct the test for the entire length of time according to manufacturer instructions. The more measurable an assessment is, the more likely it is to be accurate. Generally, with an air test, if you have greater than 3000 spores per cubic meter, then you have a mold issue. Again, mold spores are everywhere. A slightly elevated number is fine, up to an acceptable rate.

A second type of test is called a cavity sample.

"A cavity sample is unsubstantiated by research," says Richard M. Plus, the act of extracting several wall plugs in an enclosed environment can actually spread the mold even more. It can also pose a hazard to the person doing the testing, according to the IICRC (Institute of Inspection Cleaning and Restoration Certification) handbook. A professional remediation assessor would need to wear protective clothing and seal off the area before checking each cavity.

The third type of test is a swab test.

A swab sample is easier, safer, and more accurate. When taking a direct sample, the assessor will swab or tape lift a one square centimeter section.

If the amount is greater than 1000 spores per one square centimeter, that is considered elevated. Richard M. has seen cases with millions of spores on a one centimeter swab.

Hire a Qualified Assessor

Unfortunately, there is no industry standard to determine normal mold levels from problem levels. This makes it even more important to hire an experienced assessor. Not every licensed mold assessor knows what he's doing, warns Richard M. Some guys cut corners. "A lot of these testers take shortcuts. Most of these guys doing the tests don't want to hang out for 10 minutes for each sample," he explains. "But they send it to the lab, and all bets are off because they haven't followed the protocol."

Testing improperly means the lab comes back with inaccurate results. The assessor will tell the homeowner there's no mold when there really is a problem.

Richard M. recommends observing the mold assessor the entire time he is testing your property. Ask him questions and make sure he knows the right answers.

Ask him what exactly he is measuring and why. Ask him what he is looking for. How does he determine what areas to test? How is he going to test? His answers should reveal whether he is a professional or a hack. Don't hire the hack!

The Next Step

You've seen the mold with your own eyes or the tests on your property came back positive. Now what? How do you get rid of it?

Because mold absorbs and eats into whatever surface it is growing on, you can't just wipe it off. It won't work. The mold will come back, and worse, you might have actually spread it further. As the decision maker, you need to call in a restoration company to come in and get rid of the mold.

CHAPTER EIGHT
GET RID OF THAT MOLD!

A principal of an elementary school in Miami Beach called me a few months ago. He had a parent complaining that her child was coughing whenever he went into his classroom. She thought there might be mold. "There's nothing there," the principal told me. "There's no pipes or sinks or anything, how can there be mold?" But he wanted to pacify this parent. So he asked me to come and do a mold test.

Now, I couldn't do the mold test because a company that does the remediation can't be the same one that tests for the mold in the first place, due to conflict of interest laws. However, I told him I could test for water. I sent my guys to test with moisture meters and infrared cameras to see if there were any wet areas. On one of the walls, at least 10 feet of drywall, including behind the baseboard, was damp.

It turns out that the classroom had a little fish tank. A couple of weeks before, the fish tank broke. The teacher mopped it up and didn't think anything of it. There was a small water stain on the baseboard, but that was it. However, mold started to grow, and the kid who was sensitive to it started coughing and having symptoms.

I cannot stress enough the importance of drying and treating all water damage. As soon as properties are affected by fire or water, the air is destabilized and becomes a breeding ground for mold. It's very important when you have a flood or leak to get it dried as fast as possible.

If you have 20 apartments with water, you can't have a guy show up and take forever setting up in each room. If he's planning to take a few weeks to clean it all up, you're going to have mold, pure and simple. Letting wet materials sit creates the perfect atmosphere for mold to grow. Remember, mold will start to grow colonies between 24-48 hours after a water leak.

How Do I Clean It Up?

Mold doesn't clean up like dirt. Wiping it off doesn't get rid of it. If you wipe it off until you don't see it anymore, in a few days it will be back. Why? Because you failed to get rid of it in the first place. Mold absorbs into the substrate or organic material like older wood, porous material and drywall. You really can't get it out. Most of the time, you have to cut it out, and you have to contain it properly.

Just wiping mold with a cloth agitates it and causes cross contamination. When mold is disturbed, millions of spores break off and float in the air and attach themselves to other organic material. The spores are like powder or dust in the air. Each one of those spores can settle somewhere new in your property. That's how you can easily make your mold problem 10 times worse.

Although, for very small amounts of mold, your building maintenance staff can clean it very carefully with water and detergent. However, they should receive training on proper clean up methods and the importance of wearing personal protection equipment (PPE). They should wear respirator masks, gloves, and eye protection, according to OSHA guidelines.

The m aintenance s taff sh ould co ver al l un affected sur faces wit h secured plastic sheets to prevent further contamination. All areas need to be dried and cleaned completely. All work areas and everything that leaves the room should be HEPA vacuumed and cleaned with a damp cloth and detergent. Remove any contaminated materials that can't be cleaned in sealed trash bags.

If the mold infestation keeps coming back, it spreads, or the mold covers more than 10 square feet (the size of a standard sheet of drywall), call a restoration company. "The recommended protocol is to remove it," says Richard M. "That way, you never have a problem with it coming back."

How the Pros Do It

One of the main reasons why the restoration industry has grown so tremendously in the past 20 years is because we learned how to effectively control the temperature and our environment. We can seal the property so that no air goes in or out. We decide the exact temperature we want to have and when. The problem with this is that as soon as a property is affected by water or fire, it immediately becomes destabilized and therefore a grow house for mold.

Experienced restoration companies can take care of any mold case. Depending on the amount of mold, we might need to turn the affected area into a sealed chamber. It looks almost like a science or crime lab. We wear personal protective equipment to protect ourselves and to avoid contaminating other areas when we leave. This includes gloves, respirator masks, goggles, paper booties, and disposable suits.

NATIONAL WATER RESTORATION

We need to create a sealed chamber to control the environment and contain the mold spores. Professionals seal a room with large sheets of plastic and duct tape. We use a large exhaust fan with a HEPA filter to cause negative air pressure. Loosened mold spores get sucked into the vacuum instead of wandering into unaffected areas of your property. We use an air scrubber during the entire process. An air scrubber machine captures particles as small as .003 microns in size, the same size as mold spores.

We also stabilize the environment as soon as possible to inhibit further mold growth. We bring in dehumidifiers and get the dampness out of the air. Mold doesn't like that, because the spores are unable to settle and grow.

When you are cutting out sections of drywall, the concern is cross contamination. Even in a sealed room, if you have even a small hole, the mold spores will drift through it. But if you have negative pressure in the room, nothing is getting out of that hole. If we're working in a small room, we'll use a small air scrubber to create enough negative pressure. If it's a ballroom or a hotel banquet hall, then we use a very large air scrubber to get the proper negative pressure for the size of the room. With the negative pressure, the plastic sheeting will billow inwards. If the plastic flutters or billows outward, the area is not sealed and contained.

After we cut out the mold, we vacuum the walls, the floors, everything. A regular vacuum can't trap the tiny mold spores, so we use HEPA vacuums. While the air scrubber constantly filters mold spores out of air, the HEPA vacuum is more precise and deep cleans specific areas. Next, we wipe down the entire area with Microban anti-mold solution.

Even when we leave the affected room, we're careful. We'll set up another plastic chamber called the decontamination chamber. Everything in that chamber is vacuumed and wiped down. Even trash bags are double bagged with fresh bags, the tops are taped, and the outside of the bags are vacuumed.

If we notice more mold during our cleaning process, we'll bring the assessor back in to test again and rewrite the protocol. When we're finished, we retest the area to ensure the mold is gone. The air quality should be at industry standard or the same levels as outside.

Keep It or Toss It

How can you tell what can be salvaged and what needs to go? Once your property is free of mold, the last thing you want to do is bring in furniture or clothing that's still contaminated. When in doubt, throw it out.

HOUSEHOLD ITEMS

Most porous materials affected by mold will need to be trashed, including drywall.

If anything with fabric is directly affected, it needs to be thrown out, including clothing, curtains, and upholstered furniture. You can't get the mold out of the weave of the chair or sofa. You could reupholster the chair and professionally clean the wood areas of furniture, but that's expensive. For most people, it's easier to throw it away.

If there is some mold in a closet, but it is not on the clothes, send the clothes to a dry cleaner. If there's just a little spot here and there, a dry cleaner should be able to save the clothes.

Metal and glass can often be saved. Leather furniture can be cleaned. Keep in mind that in extreme environments, even glass can absorb toxins. Think of how a glass pickle jar still smells of pickles after you've washed it.

When wood is contaminated with mold, lightly sand it off, says Richard M. Wood in good condition is dense and harder for mold to absorb into.

Attempting to salvage paper items is usually a losing battle. Scan important documents and toss them.

THE AIR CONDITIONING UNIT

When mold gets into the air conditioning system, it spreads it around the whole building, and you have to clean the walls and the contents of every room in the building. Many people think that also means the whole A/C system and duct work needs to be replaced. But this is not necessarily the case.

Most of the time, air conditioners can be cleaned. We use the same concept as when we clean a room. We'll seal all the ducts with plastic. Then we attach a huge HEPA vacuum to the air conditioner handler, which will vacuum all the ducts.

But we open only one duct at a time. We use a special brush to irritate and loosen the mold. The loosened mold gets sucked right into the huge HEPA vacuum.

As soon as we finish a duct, we seal it and open a new one. Lastly, we wipe the air conditioner down with the Microban anti-mold solution.

A/C units can be cleaned. Just make sure you hire professionals who will go in and clean every duct and do their job properly.

Preventing Mold Problems

Like most things in life, some time and effort devoted to prevention can save you a host of hassles and headaches in the future. Mold especially can usually be prevented with proper maintenance and repair.

KEEP IT DRY

The number one thing you can do is fix any water or plumbing leaks immediately. Look for damp spots or areas of condensation. Richard M. explains that moisture is the number one thing mold needs to grow. But mold is not inevitable. "Kill the source of the water and dry it out," he says. "The drying process inhibits the growth of mold. But if it takes 10 days to dry, you'll have mold. Time is a very important variable."

Mold spores can begin to grow 24-48 hours after a water leak. The key is to get the property stabilized and dry within 48 to 72 hours. Contact a restoration company who will stabilize the environment with air movers and dehumidifiers. The sooner this process is completed, the less likely you will have mold problems in your property.

You also want to make sure exhaust fans are working in all of your bathrooms. The exhaust fans draw out humid air and rid the bathroom of excess moisture.

KEEP IT CLEAN

Good old-fashioned cleanliness is important when it comes to mold. Make sure you have a good custodial crew that cleans thoroughly. Pay special attention to places where there is water, such as laundry rooms, bathrooms, kitchens, air conditioning rooms, and break rooms.

KEEP THE HUMIDITY LOW

You want to make sure your building doesn't have too much humidity. An air conditioner also dehumidifies, which is why you sometimes see condensation and water around the unit.

Another thing that causes mold is stagnant air, especially with humidity. When your tenants leave for vacations and other trips, they should keep the A/C on. You want to make sure the air conditioner is constantly circulating air. In commercial buildings like condos, tenants often leave for months at a time. If they haven't run the air all summer, they'll have a mold problem when they come back.

According to Richard M., the A/C temperature should never go higher than 78 degrees. And keep humidity below 60%. The EPA recommends ideal humidity levels between 30% and 50%.

KEEP IT MAINTAINED

A regular maintenance program is critical. If the A/C unit is not maintained properly, it can cause mold. The air conditioner closet can be a big issue. The condensation and overflow in the A/C system causes mold growth. The mold grows in that closet and then circulates through every room in the house. Keep the A/C unit clean and dry. Keep air conditioning drip pans clean and make sure they are flowing properly.

Make sure your maintenance guys are changing the A/C filters according to manufacturer specifications, which is usually every 90 days. A good A/C filter can trap mold spores in the air, but if you don't change the filters, it isn't filtering any mold. A quality filter with a MERV Rating of 12 will filter mold spores.

"Especially in commercial buildings, maintenance and cleaning are the ultimate causes of most mold," Richard M. says. "It builds up over time." Basically, if you clean and maintain your property, ensure air movement and low humidity levels, and promptly clean up any water issues, you will have minimal mold issues.

In the next chapter, I will go over more ways you can protect your property through prevention. In Florida, natural disasters such as hurricanes and flooding are a reality that property managers can't afford to ignore. Chapter 9 will cover the best tips and tricks to get you prepared for the next hurricane.

CHAPTER NINE
HURRICANE PREPAREDNESS

The number one disaster threat in Florida is a hurricane, hands down. More storms hit Florida than any other state. We have the sunshine and the beautiful beaches, but we also have to deal with potential threats every year during hurricane season. Since 2000, hurricanes in Florida have caused $100 billion in damage. Of course, this is due mostly to the brutal years of 2004 and 2005, when Florida was battered by Charlie, Frances, Jeanne, and Ivan in 2004 and Dennis, Katrina, and Wilma in 2005. According to the Insurance Information Institute, 7 of the 10 costliest hurricanes in U.S. history impacted Florida.

As of this writing, the last hurricane to hit Florida was hurricane Mathew in October of 2016. The cost of damage is yet to be determined. In Florida, its not a matter of if, its a matter of when.

Don't forget, it's not just hurricanes that do damage. Storm surges cause major losses through flooding. Tropical storms and severe thunderstorms cause their share of damage. In fact, tropical storms and severe thunderstorms caused $9.6 billion in losses in the U.S. during 2015, accounting for 60% of all claims, according to the Insurance Information Institute.

When a hurricane or a severe storm does hit, you want to make sure you have your property as safe and secure as possible. As a property manager, you can take significant steps to make sure you are prepared. Don't be that guy who's left scrambling at the last second, when there's not enough time to do much to protect the property.

Be prepared. It will limit financial loss and more importantly, it can save lives. Preparation also reduces your recovery time, and faster recovery means the sooner your business is back on its feet making a full profit.

All storms are not created equal. The category of hurricane can help you determine what prep work will be required and provide you with a realistic time frame for recovery.

Types of Storms

The National Hurricane Center uses the Saffir-Simpson Hurricane Wind Scale, a 1 to 5 rating based on a hurricane's wind speed. The scale also helps estimate potential damage to property. A Category 3 or higher is considered a major hurricane.

Category	Wind Strength	Potential Damage
1	74-95 mph	Dangerous winds. Frame buildings may sustain some damage to roofs, shingles, gutters, and siding. Branches of trees will snap. Damage to power lines will result in power outages of a few days.
2	96-110 mph	Extremely dangerous winds. Frame buildings may sustain major roof and siding damage. Shallowly rooted trees will be uprooted and block some roads. Nearly total power loss with outages from several days to possibly weeks.

3	111-129 mph	Devastating damage. Frame buildings may lose part of the roof. Many trees will be uprooted and power lines will be down. Fallen trees will trap many residential areas. Power outages will last anywhere from weeks to months.
4	130-156 mph	Catastrophic damage. Buildings may sustain severe damage with loss of the roof and some exterior walls. Most trees and power poles will snap. Power outages will last weeks to months. Most of the area will be uninhabitable for weeks to months.
5	157 mph or higher	Catastrophic damage. Many buildings will be completely destroyed. Fallen trees and power poles will isolate neighborhoods. Power outages will last for weeks or months. The area will be uninhabitable, possibly for months.

Preparing for the Storm

When there's a massive hurricane bearing down on you, the last thing you want to do is rush around like a chicken with its head cut off, without a prayer or a plan. Your plan should already be in place. As the storm nears, your focus should be on two things: storing and securing.

Emergency Protective Equipment

You should already have most of the supplies that your property might need. You can pick up these items at any local hardware store. Make sure you have the following on hand: a wet vacuum, mops, garbage bags, duct tape, sandbags, plywood, gloves, batteries, flashlights, emergency generator, rags, etc.

Stockpile Plywood

You'll need to have your staff ready to board up the windows if you don't have hurricane shutters. Keep a stockpile of plywood in storage. You don't want to be the last one to the hardware store when you need 500 or more planks of wood.

Inspect the Exterior

Conduct a walkabout of the exterior of your property. Inspect roof coverings and flashings for loose shingles. Clear all storm drains of debris. Check the sump pumps and make sure everything is working properly. Look at all your trees and trim any dead limbs.

Bring in all loose items such as trash cans, lounge chairs, and anything else that can break windows when it's flying through the air at 60 miles per hour. Secure anything that can't be moved inside.

You'll also want to check the property low points. Make sure you know where flooding might be likely. Take extra steps to keep equipment out of those areas. Have sandbags on hand to minimize water intrusion into your property.

Back Up Data

Back up all electrical data off site. Move vital records off site.

Relocate Valuables

Move your valuables inventory to a safer spot or out of the path of the storm completely if you can. Relocate file boxes, computers, office machines, and other equipment to the inner-most portion of the building. Label boxes for ease of unpacking later. At a minimum, make sure all valuable equipment is moved away from windows to prevent water damage from wind-driven rain if windows break.

Remove valuable items from the ground floor in case of flooding. If you can't remove everything, then get items off the floor by placing them on desks, tables, etc.

Clear the Bric-a-brac

Clear all loose objects from desks. Take down pictures and artwork. Put away loose papers, books, etc. Cover valuables with tarps or plastic sheeting and secure with duct tape.

Turn It Off

Make sure the electricity is turned off (except for refrigeration) at the power box. Disconnect all electronic devices.

Gather Your Docs

Make sure you have your insurance policies, riders, photos, and all other important documentation either with you or in a safe, waterproof container. You should already have the restoration company's information handy. Call your insurance agent and make sure they are up to date with everything.

Find out what insurance policy to use for the storm. I've gone to buildings with a broken pipe, and they give me the information for their flood insurance. But a broken pipe is property insurance, not flood insurance. Make sure you know which policy you'll need. Know what the deductible is. I'll talk more about insurance in the next chapters.

Take Photos

Grab your camera or smart phone and snap away. Take way more pictures than you think you'll ever need. Photos are your best protection when it comes time for a claim. You want to document the condition of your property before the storm. Take pictures and video inside and outside and from several different angles.

Lock Your Doors

You don't want looters and vandals having their way with your property while the area recovers after the storm. Depending on the severity of the storm, it could be weeks before electricity is restored, so you want to secure the property while it's empty. Lock everything up and board windows, glass doors, etc.

Assign Responsibilities

At my company, I have a weekly meeting every Wednesday morning with my team. I always tell the guys that when catastrophe strikes, the reaction for most people is to run away. People want to close their eyes and pretend it's not happening, or that it won't happen. But it's our job to run toward the disaster and clean up the mess. And it's the property manager's job to think about the disaster before, during, and after it happens. It's our job to tackle the emergency. It's our job to face it and deal with it.

Most people don't want to deal with it. They don't want to think about it, and then they panic in high stress situations. But just as you need to know what to do in an emergency, your team needs to know exactly who is responsible for what and when. Never assume that they will know what to do. If you talk about it, and plan for it, and have guidelines in place, then your people are trained. They're prepared, and they are far more likely to act quickly and responsibly in the face of an emergency.

So make sure you have guidelines in place. Assign duties and responsibilities before the hurricane hits. Each staff member should know exactly what is expected of them, from the board of directors, security, and front desk personnel to maintenance, housekeeping, and administration.

Work as a team. Communication is critical. All members should have all relevant contact information. They should know how to report back to the property after the storm.

Remember, a good plan flawlessly executed is better than a perfect plan that's poorly executed. The plan doesn't have to be perfect, but you do need to have one. And it doesn't matter how awesome it is if the only copy is tucked away somewhere in your desk. Make sure every person on your team has a copy of the Emergency Readiness Program.

Returning to Your Property

After the storm, don't enter your property until it's been cleared by the fire department or local safety officials. Depending on the severity of the storm, the building may have sustained structural damage. Ruptured gas lines could cause an explosion. Other dangers include toxic sludge and bacteria in stagnant flood water and electric shock hazards.

Walkabout

When it is safe to do so, conduct another walkabout. Walk carefully around the outside of the building and check for loose wires, strange smells, and structural damage. Keep away from loose or dangling powerlines; report them immediately to the power company.

Take More Photos

Take pictures of any damage outside and inside of the property. Take pictures of all contents. Again, this is for the insurance claim. You want to document the extent of the damage before the restoration crew arrives. The burden of proof is always on the property owner. So document, document, document.

Take Safety Precautions

Only use a battery-powered flashlight inside the building. Don't use candles in case of gas leaks. Also, make sure you turn the flashlight on outside the building. The batteries could produce a spark that could ignite in a gas leak.

Never use a generator inside a property. Generators produce deadly levels of carbon monoxide and they can quickly build up in these areas and stay for hours even after the generator is off.

Depending on the amount of time the property has been vacant, uninvited guests may have moved in. Watch out for wild animals, especially snakes. Always use a stick to push away debris. Trapped rats, raccoons, and even dogs and cats will act aggressively when they are frightened.

Wear protective clothing and be cautious when cleaning up to avoid injury.

Important contact and relief information:

Ready.gov -www.ready.gov/hurricanes
Federal Emergency Management Agency - www.fema.gov
National Hurricane Center www.Floridadisaster.org/index.ASP
Red Cross www.Redcross.org/What–we-do/disaster–relief/hurricane–recovery-program
National Water Restoration www.nationalwaterrestoration.com

Whether you're dealing with storm damage or fire, water, or mold losses, you need a restoration company to help you pick up the pieces and get your property back to working order quickly. It's better to research a quality company now rather than frantically searching on your phone at 2 a.m. Chapter 10 explores the pitfalls of hiring unqualified technicians and the attributes of strong, competent companies.

CHAPTER TEN
CHOOSING THE RIGHT COMPANY

One day, we had an emergency where a 6-inch pipe burst in a condominium. There was a lake of water in the hallways. 2 of my guys ran back and forth with squeegees from one side of the hallway to the other on every single floor, pushing water into the stairwell. They were able to move the water so quickly that the carpets weren't damaged at all.

If you keep a few simple tools on hand, you can prevent further damage while you wait for a restoration company to arrive. Or, with limited flooding, you can take care of the problem yourself.

Tools to Have on Hand

- Squeegees are great for water. Have 2 or 3 squeegees on hand. You can quickly move water to a tiled area or a stairwell that won't get damaged. A mop takes far too long.
- Rags, buckets, and a few wet vacs to handle small water issues.
- Fans to help remove smoke and humidity.
- Tarps or plywood to cover broken windows or roof damage.
- Plastic sheeting to cover sensitive equipment.

Compile an inventory of tools and supplies in your emergency response plan. Make sure you include instructions on how to use the equipment and where it is located.

When dealing with water damage, you want to err on the side of caution. These days, many regular contractors and plumbers are buying a few tools and adding water restoration to their resumes. That doesn't make them qualified to do the job right.

Because water emergencies can worsen quickly, it is extremely important to get the right people the first time. Hiring inexperienced workers can end up doing way more harm than good, and the consequences from this can cost you more money and delays.

Damage Caused by Amateurs

Inexperienced people make expensive mistakes. They may open windows that should stay shut, accelerating mold growth. If they try to cut out sections of mold without an understanding of how mold develops, they can cause cross-contamination and spread the mold throughout a property. The spread of mold means a much more expensive and lengthy repair and cleaning process.

It's also important not to over-dry a property. Improper use of a dehumidifier with wooden floors can ruin the wood. If the wood doesn't dry properly, mold results. On the other hand, drying it too much causes cracking. Wood needs 12% moisture. We have special injector dry mats that suck out the moisture, but not lower than 12%.

Experienced technicians know exactly how to use the right equipment. They understand how to extract moisture from different types of materials without causing further damage. Even though the concepts seem simple, it's important to realize that using the wrong drying equipment for a job can cause a lot of damage.

Technicians know how to find hidden damage inside the walls and repair the damage. We have the necessary tools to detect moisture inside walls that look and feel dry.

A professional company will document daily moisture readings and daily humidity readings and adjust equipment needs as needed. As the property dries, they will remove unnecessary equipment. They will justify the time and cost to do the job right.

Make sure they are trained and experienced. They can have all the right tools and still not have a clue what they're doing. Just like you can have all the tools of an electrician, but that doesn't mean you should try to wire a house.

Hire the Right Company

As the decision-maker for a property, you should have 3 main objectives when you are choosing a company to restore your property. First, get a company that will get out to you fast enough. This is not a case of slow and steady wins the race. You don't want to wait 2 hours as you watch a flood of water leak downstairs while the company gets their act together. What is the company's on-time policy? My technicians get a bonus. The faster they get to a property, the higher the bonus. This means that as soon as you call our emergency line, our technicians will be running out to your location.

Second, ensure the company is properly staffed and can handle the size of your job quickly and efficiently. Some guy with a wet vacuum and some buckets in the back of his pickup truck is not going to cut it. Does the company have the equipment and manpower to get the job done right the first time? We invested in a fleet of large trucks and a ton of equipment, maximizing the amount of staff and equipment that we show up with to the job.

Third, you need to get your property up and running as fast as possible. Pick an experienced company that knows how to minimize the hassle. If they do have to cut out or demo part of the property, they should know how to do it with the least amount of mess and stress possible. A contractor should be able to come in and fix it easily.

Make sure you deal with a company that has the proper certifications and follows the industry standard, which is regulated by the IICRC (Institute of Inspection Cleaning and Restoration Certification) and the ANSI (American National Standard Institute).

Using experienced personnel the first time will prevent issues such as delayed project completion, incomplete drying leading to mold growth and health complaints, lawsuits from occupants, and denied insurance claims. A quick dry-out reduces the repair scope, which means less money out of pocket. The faster the property is restored, the faster you get back to what you do best: managing your property.

Mitigating Loss for Insurance

Insurance companies pay out $2.5 billion in water and mold claims every year. They don't want to pay out any more than they have to. Insurance companies expect property managers to take appropriate steps to prevent further damage, which they call "duties after a loss." It will be in your policy. You have to preserve and maintain the property to the best of your ability. It doesn't have to be some scary thing, but they do expect you to know what to do. They expect you to make the right call to prevent further damage.

Sometimes people don't make the right call. A guy has a leak in the house, but instead of calling a plumber, he goes on vacation and says he'll get to it when he gets back. The insurance company will claim he did not fulfill his "duties after a loss," and they will try to avoid paying. Just be proactive in terms of dealing with it. You don't have to take full responsibility, but you should try to get things under control by following the steps in this book.

I will talk more about insurance companies and walk you through the claims process in Chapter 11 and 12.

History of Water Restoration

Up until the 1950s, water restoration did not really exist. When a property was damaged by water, property managers would just wait for everything to dry and hope for the best. Of course, the water damage caused rot and mold, so they would have to rip everything out and start over.

In the 1960s, steam cleaning was invented. They would open windows and air things out. With steam cleaning, most carpets could be salvaged. In the 1970s, people started trying to actively dry wet property instead of waiting for items to dry out by themselves. They started using air movers and dehumidifiers. They realized the importance of drying areas quickly. However, the dehumidifiers couldn't dry fast enough, and most people couldn't afford the expensive equipment.

The restoration industry really took off in the 1980s when people understood that properties could be restored. Researchers came up with better technology, industry standards were established, and specialists started emerging in the field of water restoration. Now, water restoration specialists use advanced, energy-efficient technology to quickly and effectively fix water damage.

Building managers appreciate that properties can be restored in very little time, with less expense, disruption, and frustration. Insurance companies were thrilled when they realized how much money they could save by salvaging property instead of tearing everything out.

I should know. I worked in the insurance industry for nine years. Despite the horror stories you may have heard, insurance companies are generally fair and will pay out for the claims you have coverage for. As a former insurance adjuster, I know the ins and outs of dealing with insurance. In the next 2 chapters, I'll walk you through everything you need to know about making a claim and getting paid for your losses.

CHAPTER ELEVEN
KNOW YOUR INSURANCE

A few months ago, we were called into a condominium with a broken pipe on the 17th floor. Water affected 2 or 3 units on every floor down to the lobby. Over 30 units were damaged, and the cleanup took us 5 days. We sent the invoice to the manager, but the manager didn't respond. When we contacted her, she said that she got the bill, but she still didn't pay. Days and weeks passed. Finally, we went over to find out what was going on.

The property manager admitted that the building didn't have the money to pay the bill. "What about insurance?" I asked.

"Insurance covers this? Really?" she asked, completely surprised. She handed us the flood policy. "But I checked. There isn't any coverage for a broken pipe."

"Do you have another policy?" I asked her.

"Oh no, no we don't," she said. But that didn't make sense. So, she called her boss, and what do you know? She found the correct property policy. Two months after the pipe burst, we got the claim filed.

That property manager isn't alone, unfortunately. I've heard it all. But I know insurance. And you can know insurance, too. A property manager has to know which policy covers what, what the deductible is, and how to protect his or her assets.

Just like everything else in life, preparation is everything. A bit of knowledge is all it takes to avoid costly mistakes. I wouldn't necessarily call it a stress-free experience, but you can easily minimize the stress and hassle of dealing with insurance companies. In 2014, insurance companies paid out $19.7 billion in property and casualty-incurred losses in the state of Florida alone, according to the Insurance Information Institute. That makes Florida the #1 state in the country. Make sure your loss is included in that number and that the cost isn't coming from your pocket.

Know Your Policy

The policy is the contract between the property owner and the insurance company. It explains what is and is not covered. It will include the amount of coverage and any deductibles. Make sure you know the limits of coverage and any exclusions. You will probably have more than one policy, which I'll go over a bit later in the chapter. Make sure you know the differences and coverages of each one.

Types of Insurance

Law of ordinance.

There's a piece of pipe that must be replaced, but it's an old pipe, and now it isn't up to code anymore. To replace it may require replacing the entire line of piping. The insurance company will pay for that if you are covered for Law of Ordinance. I see it most often with electrical. The old wires cause a fire, then the wiring isn't up to code because it's an old property, and the whole thing needs to be replaced. Make sure you have this insurance.

Liability

Liability covers you if someone is injured on your property. If little Sally runs through your lobby and slips on the slick tile, breaking her arm, then the building's liability insurance pays for her doctor bills.

Property-casualty

This covers the structure of the building itself. Property insurance policies typically cover broken pipes, fire, lightning, hail, windstorms, smoke, explosions, vehicle damage, sprinkler leakage, and vandalism.

Sometimes additional coverage needs to be purchased for water damage or mold.

Flood

Most policies do not cover flooding. As I mentioned earlier, flood insurance is backed by FEMA. According to FEMA, the average commercial flood claim was $89,000 from 2010-2014. 25% of companies that close after catastrophic events like a flood never reopen. Don't be one of those companies. Get the proper insurance, including a separate flood insurance policy.

Content insurance

This covers belongings and personal property. Imagine taking a room and turning it upside down. Anything that would fall out is considered personal property. Renters purchase content insurance.

Loss of use

Loss of use is a homeowner policy which would provide coverage if the homeowner needed to go to a hotel during renovations. The insurance would cover the cost of the hotel.

Loss of income

This is for a business like a restaurant or hotel which covers loss of income while the business is closed.

Exclusions

Read this carefully. This is the list of what isn't covered. Common exclusions include flood, mold, sewer backup, and faulty workmanship.

Actual Cash Value versus Replacement Cost

With Replacement Cost, the insurance company will pay for a new kitchen even if it's 30-years-old. Of course, it will replace it with items of like value. Actual Cash Value equals replacement cost minus depreciation, so the insurance company may give you half of the value to go out and buy something new. If your $2000 flat-screen TV is 4 years old, the insurance company may only give you $1000 to replace it. You always want a Replacement Cost Policy.

Coinsurance

I see this with commercial property owners who are underinsured. If you have a building that is worth $800,000, but your policy is worth $400,000, you have a problem. This could happen because the agent underestimated the value of the property, or the building has appreciated in value, or you built an addition but didn't add it to your insurance coverage. The premium has been half the price all these years, but guess what, you're not fully covered.

Say you suddenly have a loss equaling $100,000 in damage. You want insurance to pay all of it, of course. But the insurance company will calculate the claim as only a percentage of the policy. If you underinsured your property by 50%, the insurance company will only reimburse you for half of the value of the damage. So they'll only write a check for $50,000, half of the $100,000 in damage.

This is an all too common problem. According to a recent study, up to 75% of properties are underinsured. I can't stress this enough. Insure your property for its correct value.

Understanding Deductibles

Basically, the deductible is the amount of money you will need to pay out of pocket before the insurance kicks in. If the amount of damage does not exceed the amount of the deductible, then you probably don't want to file a claim. For example, if you have a $100,000 claim with a $10,000 deductible, the insurance will pay $90,000. The property owner will pay $10,000 to the contractors who repair the property. If you have a claim for $9,000, you probably don't want to file a claim because you won't receive anything from your insurance company.

Condos versus homeowners

Every state is different, but in Florida, Statute 718. 111(11) states that Florida condominium associations are required to carry coverage for property and exclude from coverage all personal property within the units. This includes the floors, wall and ceiling coverings (paint and texture), and all other personal property. The role and responsibilities of the association is usually written up according to the condo docs.

It's important to educate the homeowners and new residents about what responsibilities they have and what insurance they should purchase personally. Homeowners are responsible for everything from the paint and within, including all personal property, kitchen cabinets, bathroom tile, etc. The homeowner should purchase their own homeowner's insurance.

When there is an accident in a condo or apartment building, make sure you get an incident report written up right away. A security person can write up the report and take photos. The insurance companies will rely heavily on the incident report to determine the validity of a claim.

Another thing you can do to help the homeowners of your building is to make sure the units carry their own insurance policy. Establish a maintenance program that is geared toward educating the homeowners on preventative maintenance. This will minimize losses and minimize the risk of denied claims.

Who is Responsible?

If a pipe breaks in a bathroom on the 10th floor, the owners in the unit directly below them think the people upstairs should pay for their repairs. Say I own an apartment on the 10th floor, and I see a pipe broken behind my toilet. It was an accident, so it wasn't negligence. My insurance company will pay for my loss. The water from my broken pipe damaged the bathroom cabinets in the unit below me. The person downstairs is expected to have his own policy. If he doesn't have a policy, then he is out of luck.

The building association will only take care of the drywall and common area, but that's it. The only time a homeowner will be able to get money from another homeowner is if they can prove negligence. For example, it is known that a certain type of pipe in the building is a faulty pipe, and all homeowners received an email request to replace that specific pipe, but this homeowner chose to ignore the property manager's recommendation.

Now that you know the ins and outs of your insurance policy, I'll take you through the claims process in Chapter 12.

CHAPTER TWELVE
MAKING A CLAIM

The sprinklers on the 17th floor put out the electrical fire, but now you have over 20 units damaged by fire and water. The costs to repair the property will be extensive. You survey the destruction in dismay. Now what? You need to make 2 calls: 1) Your trusted restoration company, and 2) Your insurance company.

Notify the Insurance Company Promptly

You should call the insurance company within 24 hours after a loss. You don't want to take too long, because the insurance company can send you a reservation of rights letter. This means the insurance company may investigate the claim because of the length of time between the event and the claim. If too much time passes, they may not be able to adequately investigate the case. And that gives them a valid reason to deny the claim.

This is especially true in the case of fires. Inexperienced restoration companies come in and clean up the fire damage perfectly, but they do it before the insurance and the fire department complete their investigations and write up their reports and documentation. Now the insurance company questions what, if any, damage actually happened. This is a great way to get a claim denied. Always document the damage before any clean up happens. My restoration team always takes pictures before we start the cleanup process, which adds another layer of protection.

The Insurance Claim Process

In your initial call to the insurance company, the representative will give you a claim number. While you wait for the insurance field adjuster to call you, your job is to mitigate further loss by getting the cause of the loss repaired and doing as much as you can to minimize further damage. Typically, this means calling an experienced restoration company who will document the loss and begin the cleanup process.

A field adjuster will contact you regarding the claim within 24 to 48 hours. The adjuster is your contact for the duration of the claim. He or she will visit your property to determine the cause of the loss. He is the eyes and ears of the insurance company.

He will take his own pictures and video. He'll write up a report and an estimate of the cost of the damage, and he'll submit this back to the insurance carrier. The person who receives this report is usually called a claims or desk examiner. The claims examiner will review and approve or deny the claim.

Remember, it is not the field adjuster who makes the final decisions in terms of coverage or replacement. Those decisions are made by the claims examiner sitting at his desk. If the claims examiner has any questions, he will contact the field adjuster, who will then contact you. As the property manager, you can call up the insurance company and find out which claim examiner is assigned to your file. You can call for updates and make sure the file is not just sitting in review due to an unanswered question.

Once the claims examiner reviews the claim, he makes his decision whether or not he will approve the claim.

Approved Claims

Once the examiner approves the claim, he will recommend a certain amount for payment. The insurance company will send payment with an estimate of the scope of work.

The Scope of Work

The scope of work is a detailed breakdown of every part of the job by line item. For example: remove and replace baseboard 5 linear feet, remove and replace 12 sq. ft. of drywall, remove and replace 15 sq. ft. of insulation, seal drywall and get ready for paint 120 sq. ft. of wall, paint two coats 120 sq. ft. of wall. As the property manager, you want to pay close attention and make sure every detail is included. If you notice anything missing, you can report back to your insurance adjuster. He may explain why he didn't include it in the estimate, i.e., it is a non-covered item or in his opinion, it does not have to be replaced.

The insurance company's adjuster may cut corners in his estimate and do patch-up work instead of replacement in cases that really do need replacement. I recommend getting at least 1 or 2 other contractors to bid the job so you can crosscheck the scope of work.

As a property manager, it would be wise to get the job started as soon as possible—as long as you have proper pictures and documentation of the loss to show the insurance company later.

Supplements

If more damage is discovered during the repairs, you can request an additional payment from the insurance company. For example, if you take out water-damaged drywall and discover mold, then you should document it and contact your adjuster to add it to the original claim. The claims examiner will send out another check for the new damage.

Denied Claims

Claims are denied for several reasons. I will discuss some of the more common types.

* The policy does not cover this type of loss. For example, a flood policy covers water that rises from the outside and seeps into your property, but not from fire damage or a broken pipe.

- The policy specifically excludes this type of loss. For instance, a policy states an exclusion for mold coverage.
- Denials that are due to preexisting conditions where the insurance company claims this damage was there prior to the purchase of the policy.
- Faulty workmanship denials, where the insurance company denies it because they feel that the material was cheap and not up to standard.
- Long term leakage denials where the insurance company argues that the property manager should have done more to mitigate the damage, thus denying it for negligence.
- Sometimes they may deny it when the claim was not filed in a timely manner.
- Additional reasons include failing to adequately document the loss and the state of the damage and failing to mitigate the loss to prevent further damage.

This is why it's so important to understand the coverage you have. Document everything that happened to prevent any claims of negligence and call the professionals needed to begin the mitigation of the damage immediately.

No one wants to hear that their claim was denied. However, a denied claim isn't the end of the road. You have 2 options when insurance denies a claim: 1) Mediation, and 2) Hire an attorney.

Mediation

Mediation is an informal and flexible dispute resolution process. The 2 parties, i.e., the property owner and the insurance company, are joined by a mediator. The mediator's role is to guide the parties toward their own resolution. Through joint sessions and separate sessions with both parties, the mediator helps both sides define the issues clearly, understand each other's position, and come to a resolution. Mediation is generally not binding, which means either side can walk away from the table without an agreement. Mediation is usually a fast process and can sometimes be settled on the spot.

Hire an Attorney

Your second option is to send your claim to an attorney. The attorney will review the case and check the reason for the denial of the claim. If the attorney feels you have a valid case, they will send a demand letter to the insurance company requesting payment.

You need to know that most insurance companies must cover attorney fees if the insurance company loses the case or settles. Go ahead and read that last sentence again. If you sue the insurance company and settle or win, the company is liable for *your* attorney fees. The only insurance that is not liable for those fees is flood insurance. Most commercial flood insurance policies are through FEMA, a government entity. The insurance will have a different name, but ultimately it's FEMA. They won't pay attorney fees. And nothing will move them.

Often, the attorney handling the case may not ask for money upfront if he feels you have a winning case. He will be able to collect his fees and costs from the insurance company. Make sure you hire an attorney who has experience with insurance companies so he doesn't file a lawsuit for a claim that is clearly denied in the policy.

In most cases, the insurance company will settle prior to trial. The main downside is that filing a suit is typically a lengthy process.

Disagreement Over the Claim Amount

Occasionally, there is disagreement over the value of the damage. Sometimes a property manager thinks, "Oh I have a claim, what a good time to renovate!" Don't be that guy. That's not a good way to think about a claim. Expect the insurance companies to treat you fairly, but treat them fairly in return. Look to get a fair deal, but nothing more. Insurance companies don't renovate or rebuild unless it is a total loss. They will pay for the replacement of the damage but nothing else. They will put it back to pre-loss condition. They won't likely pay for more expensive materials than you already have.

Reasonable disagreements still happen. The insurance company's contractor estimates $12,000, but your general contractor doing the same scope of work comes in with an estimate for $18,000. Your contractor may use workers who are more skilled. You want to maintain a certain standard in your property, so you want to use your contractor. But the claims examiner argues that it's not reasonable. Now what?

The Public Adjuster

You still have options. You're going to want to call a public adjuster. A public adjuster is a licensed insurance adjuster who works for you. The public adjuster will file for an "appraisal". The insurance company will send down a third-party appraiser. Your public adjuster will serve as your appraiser. They'll meet at the property and each will bring their estimate. The insurance appraiser will have the low estimate. The public adjuster, who works for you, will come in with his high estimate. They'll discuss the differences and usually meet somewhere in the middle.

If they still can't come to an agreement, then they will agree on a third-party umpire. The umpire acts as a judge, and he will make the final decision. If both appraisers cannot come to an agreement on an umpire, they go to a judge who will appoint an umpire for them.

Both your public adjuster and the appraiser will meet at the property with the umpire to go through the damages and try to reach an agreement. If they don't reach an agreement, the umpire will make a final decision on the settlement. It takes two signatures to finalize the claim: the umpire and one of the parties. It's in the interest of the umpire to ensure both parties' satisfaction. The reason for this is since both parties pay him for his services and he wants more work, it's a motivation to keep everyone happy.

When the insurance company sends out a check for the agreed amount, the public adjuster will take a certain percentage of the check. Make sure you hire a good public adjuster. Good public adjusters have positive relationships with a lot of insurance adjusters, appraisers, and umpires. He should be able to negotiate a good settlement. You want an adjuster who is aggressive, who understands insurance policies and claims, and who has long-standing relationships in the insurance industry. Check for recommendations, and remember that cheaper is not usually better. As the expression goes, "Cheap meat makes for cheap soup." An excellent public adjuster will get you a much higher settlement, thus leaving more money in your pocket.

Issuing the Check

When everyone is in agreement over the claim amount, the insurance company issues the check and sends it to the property. The insurance company doesn't get involved in the construction rebuild or cleanup. All they do is send out the funds.

If the property ownership includes a lienholder such as a mortgage company, the check will include the mortgage company's name on it; it will have to be sent out to the mortgage company for endorsements because they have an interest in the property. Some lienholders want to monitor the repairs. They will hold the money in escrow and disperse it in payments. They will usually pay a third of the funds to get the job started, and then another third once the job is partially completed, and then the last third at job completion. When the renovations are completed, the claim is closed.

Taking the Next Step

After reading this book, you are well-prepared for any disaster. You have your Emergency Readiness Program all filled out and ready to go. Your staff is trained. Your pipes are tagged. And now you've got your insurance ducks in a row, too. Go ahead and pat yourself on the back.

But wait, there's 1 more step. You want to have a great restoration company at the ready. A good restoration company will not only restore your property professionally and efficiently; they will help you document your claims. At National Water Restoration, we go the extra mile and actually file your claim for you.

Actually, my company goes the extra mile in everything we do. In Chapter 13, I'll explain why National Water Restoration is the company you want in your lineup the next time something goes horribly wrong.

CHAPTER THIRTEEN

THE COMPANY YOU KEEP

I am the owner of National Water Restoration, one of the largest restoration companies in Florida. We do water, fire, and mold emergency cleanup. We specialize in large losses. In the past year, we have serviced over 2000 properties, and we are the preferred vendor of the largest management companies in Florida. In 2015, one of our employees was awarded the key to the City of Surfside as a recognition for the hard work and dedication that we provide.

From my experience, property managers and chief engineers share 3 major concerns when faced with a large emergency:

1) Getting a company to come out fast enough.
2) Making sure the company is properly staffed with the right amount of equipment to get the job done right the first time.
3) Getting the building restored as quickly as possible with minimum disruptions and hassles.

At National Water Restoration, we solve these problems:

1) We implemented a strict company policy when it comes to response time. The faster the technician shows up to the job location, the bigger the bonus they receive. As soon as you

call our hotline, our technicians are running out to your location.

2) We've invested in large trucks and lots of equipment, maximizing the amount of staff and equipment that we bring to the job. We keep a huge inventory of equipment in each truck to ensure we can tackle any size job and begin work immediately upon arrival.

3) We begin the restoration process during the dry-out by doing 2 things: a) minimizing damage instead of tearing out the drywall that is wet, we dry it and b) only if needed, doing a controlled demolition. We cut out drywall in a way that it can be put back immediately. This solves the issue contractors sometimes face when they get to a job and then have to recut the drywall in order to repair.

My staff knows I am constantly bringing up our motto: "Excellence, Integrity, Reliability." Our motto personifies who we are and what we stand for as a company. I also instill in my staff a sense of responsibility for every job, which is what decision-makers expect from us.

My experienced and certified technicians are trained in the latest techniques. We use the most advanced tools and equipment available in the industry.

As a property manager, you want your staff to have a restoration company on call. That way, whoever is on duty at your property can call in the reinforcements immediately. They don't have to hastily scan through their phone while a lake of water on the 10th floor leaks into new units with every passing minute. Pick your restoration company while the sun is shining, and you'll be the one that's already back on your feet after the emergency hits.

Large losses are what we specialize in. The great thing about working with us is that after you call us once, you will always call us back. Call 1-877-933-7924 and choose us as your preferred restoration company. We offer our services each and every day, 24 hours a day, 365 days a year.

Now that you've read this book, and you're are equipped with the right tools and knowledge, you can be confident that when you have to face a fire, water, mold, or storm emergency you'll be able to take a leading role. The owners and tenants that have entrusted you with their property will truly consider you their hero.

> "National Water is an excellent restoration company that takes pride in their professional services and the comfort of their clients. When working with them, they were always on time, organized, and very courteous . . . I would highly recommend this company to anyone in need of remediation, restoration, and water extraction services."
>
> -Malaga Towers Condominium Association, INC.
> Hallandale, FL

> "National Water Restoration's technicians were very friendly and professional. National Water Restoration made it comfortable not only for our employees but for all the passengers and guest at the airport. They are very professional, and their prices are very competitive, we would use National Water Restoration any time we have another emergency."
>
> Cityworks Construction LLC
> Miami, FL

"I have worked with National Water Restoration on several big restoration projects, and found them to have a great response time, and impeccable customer service; they are extremely efficient in remediation services, and emergency response."

Plaza of the Americas
Sunny Isles Beach, FL

"I have worked with National Water Restoration on a number of large restoration projects on which they have always responded very quickly and efficiently to provide immediate emergency service to any situation we have encountered. Their technicians and staff are always ready to assess any type of remediation…"

Plaza Construction
Miami, FL

"It has been our experience on several occasions with the ongoing construction in a 40 plus year-old property that they have gone above and beyond the scope that was agreed on. Most recently they were instrumental on restoration of the Beachcraft Restaurant fire on opening day where they worked diligently to get the restaurant back on track."

Roney Palace
Miami Beach, FL

AUTHOR'S BIO

Jonathan Fish is a graduate of Thomas Edison State University in New Jersey. He started out as an insurance adjuster in 2003, and in 2010 he began working in the restoration industry.

With his many years of claims experience, he opened up National Water Restoration, which now serves Florida. Under his leadership, National Water Restoration has assisted thousands of properties damaged by water, fire, mold and storm.

He is also the founder of the Widows Foundation, a non-profit organization dedicated to supporting families coping with the loss of the breadwinner.

Mr. Fish has lived in Florida with his wife for 16 years. They have four children. Between raising a family and running a thriving business, Mr. Fish also enjoys traveling, kite surfing, and many of the water sports available in South Florida.

You may contact Jonathan Fish at:
His office number (877) 933- 7924
Or by email: jonathan@nationalwaterrestoration.com
Or visit www.nationalwaterrestoration.com